*Capital Libraries and Librarians*

# Capital Libraries and Librarians

A BRIEF HISTORY OF
THE DISTRICT OF COLUMBIA
LIBRARY ASSOCIATION
1894–1994

BY JOHN Y. COLE

Library of Congress

Washington 1994

JOHN Y. COLE, a librarian and historian, has been on the staff of
the Library of Congress since 1966 and director of the Center for
the Book in the Library of Congress since it was established in 1977.

Library of Congress Cataloging-in-Publication Data

Cole, John Young, 1940–
    Capital libraries and librarians : a brief history of the District
of Columbia Library Association / by John Y. Cole.
        p.   cm.
    Includes bibliographical references (p.   ).
    ISBN 0-8444-0837-9
——— Copy 3 z663 .c23   1994
    1. District of Columbia Library Association—History   2. Library
science—Washington (D.C.)—Societies, etc.—History.   I. Title.
z673.D62c65   1994
020'.6'232753—dc20                          94-12277
                                            CIP

COVER: The device of the District of Columbia Library Association, adopted
in 1965, is based on the George Washington family shield as adapted by
James Thackara and John Vallance and first imprinted on a map of
the City of Washington engraved in 1792.

# TABLE OF CONTENTS

# INTRODUCTION
⚜

WASHINGTON, D.C., is the library and information center of America. According to the *Washington Area Library Directory* published by the District of Columbia Library Association in 1992, there are more than 850 libraries and information centers in the Washington, D.C., metropolitan area. It is estimated that approximately one-fifth of the library resources—collections and professional librarians—in the United States are here; so are dozens of large research organizations and hundreds of smaller research institutes and offices.

The Library of Congress, the Smithsonian Institution, and the National Archives are probably the most widely-known research institutions in the capital, but the Washington, D.C., metropolitan area is also the home of the National Library of Medicine, the National Agricultural Library, the Folger Shakespeare Library, Dumbarton Oaks, the National Institutes of Health, more than sixty federal libraries, plus the District of Columbia Public Library, a system with twenty-five branches, and twelve universities and colleges—including the American University, Catholic University of America, the George Washington University, Georgetown University, and the University of Maryland. The Association of Research Libraries and the Special Libraries Association have their headquarters here.

The presence of so many federal libraries has shaped the library and information scene in Washington and helped define the activities of the District of Columbia Library Association (DCLA). What DCLA member Adelaide R. Hasse said in a 1936 talk about libraries in the capital is still true: the libraries of Washington "owe not only their existence but their character to the requirements of the men and women who are shaping the nation's policy and to a large extent national development." Yet, from the beginning, DCLA officers have taken steps to include librarians from all types of libraries in the organization. Moreover, DCLA has played a key role in local library development: the promotion of the idea of a free public library in Washington was one of its earliest and most important efforts.

When it was established in 1894, DCLA became one of the first local library associations in the United States. Since its creation, it has helped unify the many and diverse groups of libraries and librarians in the Washington, D.C., area. Among the nation's library associations, DCLA has played a unique role in increasing awareness about federal libraries and librarianship. Through its meetings, and especially through its publications, it has provided information and improved access to the rich and unique library resources of the nation's capital. In collaboration with the American Library Association (ALA), especially after ALA established its Washington office in 1945, DCLA has helped educate librarians and citizens about the importance of legislative action on behalf of all types of libraries. Along the way, many national figures have participated in DCLA's programs and used it as a platform for expressing their views about libraries and their role in the life of the nation.

# CHAPTER ONE

*Washington, D.C., in the Gilded Age*

The EXPANSION of the United States and its federal government in the years following the Civil War transformed the city of Washington: it became a growing and more liveable metropolis, a center for the federal bureaucracy and for tourists, and, increasingly, a city of scientific and intellectual accomplishment.

Between 1880 and 1900, Washington's population grew from about 177,000 to more than 278,000. The first telephones appeared in 1878, the first street light was turned on in 1881, and electric streetcars began operating in 1888. Frederick Law Olmsted began redesigning the Capitol grounds in the 1870s. The length of the Mall nearly doubled between 1882 and 1900 as the Army Corps of Engineers reclaimed the tidal flats west and south of the Washington Monument. Congress set land aside for the National Zoo in 1889 and established Rock Creek Park in 1890 for the "benefit and enjoyment of the people of the United States." The construction industry boomed and many impressive buildings were completed—some after many years of work.

The new structures included the colorfully bricked U.S. National Museum (1881), which is now the Smithsonian's Arts and Industries Building; the Washington Monument (1884), which became the world's tallest structure; in 1887, the immense Pension Building (now the National Building Museum) on F Street between 4th and 5th Streets, NW, at the time the largest brick (more than 15 million) structure ever constructed; also in 1887, the Army Medical Museum and Library, which was located where the Hirshhorn Museum now stands; and, in 1888, the ornate State, War, and Navy Building, now the Old Executive Office Building.

A separate building for the Library of Congress, which had outgrown its rooms in the Capitol, was authorized in 1886. When it opened to the public in 1897, the imposing beaux arts structure was the largest library building in the world. The Romanesque and granite-towered Post Office Building on Pennsylvania Avenue was completed in 1899. As the city's centennial in the year 1900 neared, plans were formed

An engraving from *Frank Leslie's Illustrated Newspaper*, 24 May 1884, shows members of the League of American Wheelmen cycling down Pennsylvania Avenue. The Capitol building, the first home of the Library of Congress, is in the background.

to resurrect L'Enfant's name and original plan as the basis for a new, monumental capital city.

Simultaneously, Washington flowered as a center of intellectual, scientific, and professional activity. Optimism, nationalism, and the increasing specialization of knowledge fueled the expansion of institutions such as the U.S. Geological Survey, the Army Medical Museum and Library, the Department of Agriculture, the Smithsonian Institution, and the Library of Congress. The new federal bureaus brought scientists and cultural leaders to Washington, and a new cosmopolitanism. A unique feature of Washington society in the 1880s, noted correspondent Frank G. Carpenter of the *Cleveland Leader*, was that:

The new Library of Congress Building was almost complete when the photo-graph (*top*) was taken on 22 May 1895. The popular Neptune Fountain in front of the new building was completed in February 1898.

the most important and successful men in all branches of activity come here. Instead of there being one lion to roar at a party, there may be twenty or thirty. So many men and women of brains and brilliance give Washington gatherings a sparkle that is found nowhere else, except perhaps in the capitals of Europe.

The "brains and brilliance" of the new Washingtonians stimulated the creation of a large array of local intellectual, scientific, and social organizations. Individuals banded together for professional, civic, and educational purposes, and for personal self-improvement. The organizations they formed included the Philosophical Society (1871), the Cosmos Club (1878), the Literary Society (1879), the Anthropological Society (1879), the Biological Society (1880), the National Geographic Society (1888), the Geological Society of Washington (1893), and the Columbia Historical Society (1894). Many of the members of these new groups helped create the new library association.

The new organization was born in the midst of a national depression and fears of labor unrest. "Coxey's Army" of unemployed workers had marched on the city in the spring of 1894 and demonstrators were arrested on the steps of the U.S. Capitol on 1 May. On the last day of May, potential members of "a library club to promote intercourse among persons engaged in library work in Washington" were invited to an organizational meeting on 6 June.

The organizers of Washington "library club," which would officially be named the Library Association of Washington City, were quite aware of the national economic depression and of Coxey's Army; in fact, they could not avoid the Army, since it was camped on the Mall between the Washington Monument and the Capitol. But the motivations of the organizers were primarily local, not national. And there was a single local cause that focused its initial efforts: unlike Boston, Chicago, and many other cities, Washington—the nation's capital—did not have a free public library.

# CHAPTER TWO

# Creating DCLA

THE MODERN library movement dates from 1876 when a convention of American librarians, meeting in Philadelphia during the Centennial Exposition, formed the American Library Association (1876). The energetic Melvil Dewey, one of the guiding forces behind the creation of the ALA, applied his organizational skills again in 1883 when he formed the New York Library Club, the first of many similar local library organizations to be established around the country. The Southern California Library Club, the Massachusetts Library Association, the Indiana State Library Association, and the Chicago Library Club were all created in late 1891.

The Chicago World's Columbian Exposition of 1893, like the Philadelphia Exposition, encouraged both nationalism and the growth of professional associations. The ALA and many other organizations held their annual meetings in conjunction with the Chicago Fair, and six librarians from Washington City participated in the ALA's annual meeting in Chicago. The next year, five of them (Ainsworth Rand Spofford, Edward J. Farquhar, Weston Flint, B. Pickman Mann, and Henderson Presnell) became charter members of the new Library Association of Washington City.

The call for the new organization of librarians in the nation's capital was extended on 31 May 1894. The invitation pasted in a scrapbook in the DCLA Archives reads:

> You are invited to attend a meeting to be held on Wednesday afternoon June 6 at 4:30 o'clock, at the Columbian University, for the formation of a library club, to promote intercourse among persons engaged in library work in Washington.

The invitation lists ten individuals who wanted to create the organization:

Ainsworth Rand Spofford, Librarian of Congress
Charles C. Darwin, librarian, Geological Survey
Edward J. Farquhar, librarian, Patent Office
Mrs. H. L. McL. Kimball, librarian, Treasury Department
William P. Cutter, librarian, Department of Agriculture
Andrew H. Allen, librarian, Department of State
Howard L. Prince, librarian, Patent Office
Oliver L. Fassig, librarian, Weather Bureau

W. H. Lowdermilk, bookseller

Cyrus Adler, librarian, Smithsonian Institution

Was there a single instigator? The answer is unclear. At the fortieth anniversary meeting in 1934, Washington librarian Adelaide Hasse speculated that W. P. Cutter played that role. But Cutter, in a letter written for the anniversary occasion, took no personal credit. In fact, he stated that Miss Josephine Clark, a trained librarian who at the time was his assistant at the Department of Agriculture, was "really the founder of the Association." If this is true, her influence was entirely behind-the-scenes, because her name is not on the invitation.

However it happened, there is no doubt that the most influential name on the invitation was that of sixty-nine-year old Ainsworth Rand Spofford, the distinguished Librarian of Congress.

Twenty-three librarians attended the 6 June meeting at Columbian University at 15th and H Streets, NW (Columbian University became the George Washington University in 1904). The proceedings of the meeting were well-orchestrated. Cyrus Adler of the Smithsonian Institution called the session to order and recognized Edward Farquhar, who moved that a temporary organization be established with Mr. Adler serving as chairman and Mr. Fassig as secretary. This was agreed. Messrs. Cutter and Farquhar emphasized that, even though federal librarians dominated the Washington library scene, the new association was to be open to all Washington librarians.

Next, Mr. Darwin introduced Spofford as "one whom we all delight to honor" and the senior and best-known librarian in the city took the floor. Mr. Spofford lent his endorsement to the idea of the association in his deliberate, albeit indirect manner: "It is always a pleasure to me to help forward any good cause, and this certainly is one. So far as my engrossing labors permit, I will give it every assistance in my power." He again emphasized that the new group should be open to all librarians, and read a letter from the librarian of Catholic University who regretted he could not attend the meeting but pledged his support for the idea and future cooperation. In a brief digression, Spofford described a library matter very much on his mind: the problems created by the flood of copyright materials still pouring into the Library of Congress's rooms in the Capitol Building while the Library awaited the completion of its new building across the plaza from the Capitol.

Coming back to the topic at hand, he commented "the simpler our association is made, the better," a succinct statement that undoubtedly contributed to his being named chairman of the proposed association's organization committee.

Three members of the committee (Cutter, Fassig, Kimball) met with Spofford at his home near 16th and Massachusetts Avenue, NW, on Monday night, 11 June. The group drafted a constitution and issued a call for a formal organizational meeting, which would take place only four days later, on 15 June. The invitation was sent to forty-four librarians throughout the city. The majority represented federal agencies, but invitations were also sent to the librarians of the Carroll Institute, Catholic University, Georgetown

Ainsworth Rand Spofford, Librarian of Congress (1864–1897) and first president of the District of Columbia Library Association (1894–1895), was photographed at his desk in the Library's quarters in the Capitol.

LIBRARY ASSOCIATION
OF WASHINGTON CITY

HANDBOOK

WITH NOTES ON
LIBRARIES IN WASHINGTON

WASHINGTON, D. C.
1897

The first DCLA publication, *Handbook; with Notes on Libraries in Washington*, which appeared in 1897, could already describe sixty-one libraries in the area.

University, the Masonic Library, the Medical Society of D.C., the Peabody Library and several other nongovernmental libraries.

The short notice for the meeting seriously diminished attendance; for example, neither Spofford nor Cyrus Adler, the temporary chairman, could be there. Twenty-two librarians were present, however,

and Mr. Fassig, the temporary secretary, called the meeting to order. W. H. Lowdermilk, one of the signers of the initial invitation and the city's leading antiquarian bookseller, was chosen to chair the meeting. One decision was easy to make: all forty-four recipients of the invitation to the meeting would be considered charter members of the new organization.

After a lengthy discussion, the constitution prepared by the committee on organization "was adopted practically as reported." The object of the new Library Association of Washington City was broadly conceived: "to promote intercourse among librarians and all interested in library work in Washington City and vicinity and to further library interests in general." There was an exclusivity in the early years; current members could nominate "any person interested in library work" for membership, but that individual had to be approved by a vote of the executive committee. The dues were a dollar a year. A "no surprise" slate of officers was elected:

President: Ainsworth Rand Spofford
First Vice President: Cyrus Adler
Second Vice President: W. H. Lowdermilk
Secretary-Treasurer: Oliver L. Fassig
Other members of the executive committee:
William P. Cutter, Charles C. Darwin,
Mrs. H. L. McL. Kimball.

The executive committee of the new Library Association met at Mr. Spofford's home on 10 October to plan the first meetings and future directions. Columbian University was established as the principal place for the meetings, which would take place once a month, on Wednesdays, October through May.

Six areas of immediate professional interest were established by the executive committee; each was of a practical nature and primarily of local interest. They were: 1) preparing a union list of periodicals held by Washington libraries; 2) developing a system of mutual exchange of duplicates and other books; 3) interlibrary loan among District of Columbia libraries; 4) formulating methods of processing and caring for maps; 5) formulating methods of arranging and indexing public documents; and 6) assisting in the movement to establish a free public library system in Washington.

The first regular meeting, attended by twenty-three people, took place on 24 October in the Directors' Room at Columbian University. President Spofford delivered an inaugural address, thanking the association for honoring him and then describing the attributes of the profession of librarianship. Committees were appointed for the "practical work" needed in each of the areas of professional interest established by the executive committee. Those present were then asked to describe the activities of their own libraries, beginning a tradition of annual "experience" meetings that was incorporated into the association's programs.

The constitution of the new association was amended in 1901, changing the name of the organization to the District of Columbia Library Association. A reorganization in 1926–1927 resulted in repeal of the constitution and the incorporation, on 10 February 1927, of the organization under a new set of by-laws. The receipt for the $2 incorporation fee is in the DCLA archives. The association's objective, according to the new by-laws, was "to promote the welfare of libraries and library workers in Washington City and vicinity" and the organization was now open "to any person interested in libraries." The annual dues were raised to $1.50 and a life membership cost $25.

# CHAPTER THREE

# A Public Library for the District of Columbia

THE MOST important action taken at the 24 October 1894 meeting was the creation of action committees; the need for a free public library in Washington was at the top of the agenda. Washington, a city of 250,000 and filled with libraries, had no municipal library for the use of the general public. The lack of local self-government made the creation of such an institution difficult—as did the presence of the Library of Congress, which some members of Congress (and many members of the public) felt should serve as both a congressional and a local library.

Theodore W. Noyes, the president of the Washington Board of Trade and associate editor of the Washington *Evening Star*, led the movement for a public library and Librarian of Congress Spofford endorsed the idea in newspaper interviews and in testimony before Congressional committees. A bill introduced in Congress in 1891 had failed, but a new campaign was started in 1894. A March 1894 report by the Public Library Committee of the Washington Board of Trade, chaired by Noyes, links libraries, reading, and self-improvement:

> There are over fifty-two libraries in the District, each containing over one thousand volumes, and not one of them is a free lending library, with a reading-room open at night for the benefit of the general public. Such an institution is the most urgent need of the National Capital. Viewing this ocean of more than a million books, spread tantalizingly before them, the workingmen, the school children, the Government clerks, the great mass of the citizens of Washington, thirsty for the knowledge which comes from reading, may well exclaim with the Ancient Mariner: "Water, water everywhere, nor any drop to drink!"

A bill for the establishment of a "free public and departmental library and reading room in the District of Columbia" was approved in the U.S. House of Representatives in July 1894. The library was to be

Civic-minded Theodore W. Noyes, associate editor of the Washington *Evening Star*, was a principal founder of the District of Columbia Public Library and the chairman of its board of trustees for forty years.

of the State Department. *The Library Journal* reported that "all of these gentlemen are earnest advocates of the cause" and that "a vigorous campaign will doubtless be waged this winter."

In fact, General Greely was a leader of the cause and, in collaboration with his fellow committee members and other prominent Washingtonians, including Theodore Noyes, he spearheaded a plan that eventually worked. While continuing the campaign in Congress for a publicly-supported library, a privately-supported subscription library would be established. Its collections would form the basis of the new public library once Congress, impressed by this show of good faith by library enthusiasts and the citizens of Washington, created such an institution.

General Greely presented the plan at the second regular meeting of the new library association, held on 21 November 1894, and requested individual subscriptions. He continued his steady work and reported to the association again on 19 December. By April 1895, more than $10,000 had been pledged, and the Library Association of Washington City helped arrange a meeting of subscribers to the proposed Washington City Free Library that was held on 26 April. The new library was incorporated on 1 July, with General Greely as its president. Rooms were rented in the McLean Building at 1517 H Street, NW, near the corner of Vermont and H Streets, NW, and an eight-member library committee, which included several members of the Library Association, began accessioning, classifying, cataloging, and arranging the books. The citizens of the city donated more than 1,700 vol-

located in the new Post Office Building then being planned. It would be funded jointly by the federal government and the District of Columbia, and stocked largely by duplicate materials transferred from the departmental libraries and the Library of Congress. Each of these provisions was controversial, however, and the bill became stalled in congressional debate.

The new Library Association of Washington City assigned a "strong committee" to carry out "this important work," consisting of Brigadier General A.W. Greely, chief signal officer of the U.S. Army, who was in charge of the War Department Library (chair); Ainsworth Rand Spofford; and A. H. Allen, librarian

Brigadier General A. W. Greely was in charge of the War Department Library, chair of DCLA's committee to help create a D.C. public library, and president of the public library's "stalking-horse"—the Washington City Free Library.

Washington's first public library, three-quarters of whose books came from the Free Library, occupied rented quarters at 1326 New York Avenue, NW, from late December 1898 until early January 1903.

The District of Columbia Public Library opened its handsome new beaux arts building on Mount Vernon Square to the public in 1903. The Library's cataloging department is shown hard at work two years later.

umes to the enterprise, which opened its doors to the public on 6 January 1896.

The library was an immediate success: 2,200 books were loaned in January, 4,900 in February, and 4,000 during the first three weeks of March. General Greely, who had persuaded many prominent Washingtonians to subscribe, kept up the pressure. In a report dated 20 March 1896, he related that a new bill to create a public library was still pending in Congress, and that, even if the bill should pass, there would be a delay in making appropriated funds available. Nevertheless, in the meantime:

> The men and women who have so liberally contributed to the opening of the Washington City Free Library, and have initiated an institution that has stimulated Congress to its educational duty to the public, have every reason to be proud.

Finally, on 3 June 1896, Congress approved the creation of the District of Columbia free public library—but no appropriation would become available until 1 July 1898. The Washington City Free Library continued to serve citizens until 15 July 1898, when it closed its doors. Its collections became the core of the new municipal library, which leased a building at 1326 New York Avenue, NW, and opened in late 1898.

·Library advocate and Washington Board of Trade president Theodore W. Noyes became chairman of the new board of trustees—a position he held until his death fifty years later. His work done, General A. W. Greely stepped aside. Librarian of Congress Spofford provided continuity with DCLA, however, for he became a trustee and chairman of the public library's book committee. Moreover, from 1898 until his death in 1908, Spofford "revised and approved" practically all book purchases for the new institution.

The ties between DCLA and the Public Library of the District of Columbia have remained close through the years. The first librarian, Weston Flint (1898–1904), was a charter member of the association, and kept its members up-to-date about the infant library's activities. DCLA even paid for several reference books and periodical subscriptions in the early years. In 1899, after Andrew Carnegie offered to fund a new library building if Congress would provide a site and suitable maintenance, DCLA members supported the campaign for a Mount Vernon Square location at 7th and New York Avenue, NW. Not surprisingly, after the monumental beaux arts classical building was opened in 1903, it provided headquarters and meeting space for the association.

George F. Bowerman, librarian of the District of Columbia Public Library from 1904–1940, served as DCLA president in 1906–1907. His successor, Clara W. Herbert, was DCLA president from 1925–1927, and the first woman to serve as president. In later years, six other D.C. Public Library staff members became association president.

# CHAPTER FOUR

# Professional Interests and Activities, 1894–1945

REVIEWING the archives of the District of Columbia Library Association, one is struck by the earnestness and enthusiasm of the association's leaders during the early years. The seriousness of the founders and their wide-ranging interests made DCLA a vital organization during its first two decades, albeit from our perspective the leaders constituted a relatively small and elite group of mostly—but not entirely—white males. Social issues have never been a major concern of DCLA as an organization. It should be noted, however, that the reading rooms of the Library of Congress and the D.C. Public Library have always been open to individuals of all races—almost the only public places, in addition to trolleys, buses, and Griffith Stadium, in pre-World War II Washington, D.C., where racial segregation was not practiced.

From 1894 to 1903, most meetings were held at Columbian University. The handsome new Public Library building on Mount Vernon Square was the usual meeting site from 1904 until 1921. In 1922, when the association increased the number of social meetings, the Dodge Hotel Tea House at 20 E Street, NW, became the preferred location. Throughout this period, there were occasional visits to other institutions (e.g., to the library of the Scottish Rite Temple on 24 February 1897, and to the Carroll Institute on 17 April 1901) and occasional "excursions" to places such as Great Falls (three times), the Soldiers Home, Marshall Hall, Annapolis, and Camp Meade, which was reached by trolley car. In 1927, DCLA began holding its meetings in different locations throughout the city. New buildings were especially popular. For example, the National Archives building, opened in 1935, was a favored site from 1936–1940. Dumbarton Oaks hosted many meetings from 1941–1952.

Membership reached 168 in 1904, but then leveled off and, about 1914, DCLA went into a period of decline and stagnation that lasted until about 1925, even though there were important accomplishments during these years. By 1916, it had become difficult to recruit both officers and members and, symbolically, for a short period the association's constitution and by-laws were lost. At a meeting on 14 February 1917, there even was discussion about whether the organization should be dissolved.

The solution to the dilemma came from the

members themselves. The answer was fewer and less formal program meetings, with a reduction in the number of papers that were presented and more discussion of current issues. Members were to have more opportunities to become better acquainted through more social occasions and, in general, there was to be more active membership participation. The constitution was located and amended to this effect. Membership increased to 165 in 1920, and a turn-around (one of several in DCLA's history) was under way.

Between 1894 and 1945, an average of six program meetings were held each year. Before the (modest) membership rebellion of 1917–1918, most of the programs consisted of formal papers, followed by discussion. Beginning in 1918, presentations on particular topics were mixed with reports on developments at government libraries, short book reviews, and questions and answers about library work.

In October 1894, in addition to the committee for the public library, DCLA's officers established committees to investigate and report on five other topics of special interest: a union list of periodicals; the exchange of duplicate materials; interlibrary loan; maps; and public documents. Little seems to have happened regarding duplicate materials, even though there was discussion and some confusion about whether or not the proposed new public library would depend on surplus materials from government libraries (it did not). A program on "The Care of Maps" by F. H. Parsons of the Library of Congress on 27 March 1895, apparently satisfied those interested in the topic, for the next program on cartography ("Map Making and Map Values in the United States") was not held until 18 March 1908.

Many of today's DCLA members will sympathize with the advice given in 1944 "to future program makers" by George F. Bowerman, who was writing on the occasion of DCLA's fiftieth anniversary. He advocated more programs "of wide cultural interest, including those on literary and artistic subjects and current affairs topics." He felt that such programs appealed to both of DCLA's principal membership groups: federal librarians and public librarians. In Dr. Bowerman's view, the problem was that "programs that appealed primarily to the personnel of the Library of Congress and the departmental libraries often did not mean much to Public Library members and, conversely, when programs that were of vital interest to Public Library personnel were staged, it was often felt that they were of slight interest to the other group."

In fact, Dr. Bowerman, speaking for the public library side, could have made another point. Bibliographic, technical, and collection related topics appear more frequently on the DCLA program than issues that might have more direct appeal to public libraries and librarians. And the Library of Congress, through 1945, does tend to dominate.

Apart from the success of individual programs, the attempt to appeal to DCLA's varied membership meant that the range of programs was exceptionally broad—and sometimes surprising. To choose two early examples that do not fit easily into any categories: "Unconscious Humor in Typography" was bibliographer H. Carrington Bolton's topic in an

11 November 1899 presentation, and on 11 October 1916, in the midst of the association's first bout with organizational difficulties and unhappiness with its programs, members heard a presentation by Percy Hickling on "Mental Hygiene for Library Workers."

The summary of professional interests and activities that follows is selective, concentrating on the major areas of interest during DCLA's first half century, from 1894–1945. DCLA members will recognize many of the issues (and problems) that are discussed by today's "interest groups." And considering George Bowerman's concern in 1944, it is somewhat ironic that DCLA's activities after 1945 generally became less scholarly and more practical, emphasizing legislative action, access to resources, and other issues that related directly to library service.

## A Union List of Periodicals

The committee, chaired by Smithsonian librarian Cyrus Adler, investigated union lists of periodicals developed in New York City, Boston, Philadelphia, and Baltimore. Adler presented a preliminary report at the meeting of 24 April 1895, which also featured a paper by President Spofford on "Periodicals of the Past in the District." The findings of the questionnaire and committee recommendations were referred to the executive committee on 29 May 1895, and helped pave the way for the eventual publication, in 1901 by the Library of Congress, of the 315-page *A Union List of Periodicals, Transactions, and Allied Publications Currently Received in the Principal Libraries of the District of Columbia*, compiled under the direction of A. P. C. Griffin. On 27 February 1896, H. Carrington Bolton presented a proposal for a checklist of scientific periodicals. Allan B. Slauson of the Library of Congress made a presentation, on 3 March 1900, about the opening of the Library's periodicals reading room. Interest in periodicals and union lists continued in later years, but without the intensity shown in the association's first decade.

## Interlibrary Loan

On 27 February 1895, Henderson Presnell presented a report from his "Committee on the Practice of Lending Books by Government Libraries in Washington." Questionnaires sent to thirty libraries (and returned by twenty-six) indicated relatively liberal interlibrary loan policies, except for books in reference collections. The survey information was useful to Librarian of Congress Herbert Putnam in seeking approval to initiate interlibrary loan at the Library of Congress in 1901. On 21 December 1904, Ernest C. Richardson spoke on the topic "Traveling Students vs. Traveling Books." William Warner Bishop of the Library of Congress discussed the topic at a program on 17 November 1909, and then it disappeared from the agenda at association meetings.

## Public Documents

Located in the seat of government publishing and the home of so many federal libraries, Washington librarians naturally had a strong interest in all aspects of public documents, from creation to distribution and use. More than twenty DCLA programs were devoted to the topic between 1894 and 1945. The first, on 30 January 1895, featured DCLA member John G. Ames, chief of the Documents Division, Department of the Interior, and compiler of the *Comprehensive Index of Publications of the United States Government, 1881–1893*, discussing the recently approved law regarding the printing, binding, and distribution of public documents. The law provided for the appointment of the first Superintendent of Documents, which occurred on 26 March 1895 with the naming of DCLA member Francis A. Crandall to the post, and the creation of a Public Documents Library. Foreign documents were also of interest to DCLA members. For example, on 12 February 1908, Smithsonian librarian Cyrus Adler presented a brief historical account of the Smithsonian's international exchange service.

## THE NEW LIBRARY OF CONGRESS BUILDING

DCLA members were keenly interested in the plans for the new Library of Congress Building (today known as the Jefferson Building), which was under construction when the association was established. President Spofford gave a paper, "The Functions of a National Library," at the 27 November 1895 meeting. The new building was described at the 25 November 1896 meeting by Superintendent of Construction (and DCLA member) Bernard Green, who was preparing

members for a special tour of the building on 6 December. More than seventy-five members joined Green for the two-hour tour of what was touted as the "largest, costliest, and safest" library building in the world.

The old library in the Capitol was closed on 31 July 1897 and during the next three months more than eight hundred tons of books, maps, manuscripts, pieces of music, and other materials were transported across the Capitol's east plaza into the new structure. On 27 October 1897, four days before the new building opened to the public, Green described the move to DCLA members and related seeing what no one in his generation had ever witnessed: the old library in the Capitol "with empty shelves, the room swept and dusted, and Mr. Spofford seated with his hat on, resting." Green, who became Superintendent of Building and Grounds once the Library of Congress building opened, also served from 1899–1902 as superintendent of construction for the Carnegie building of the Public Library of the District of Columbia.

## BIBLIOGRAPHY

Bibliographic work in all subjects was of interest to DCLA members in the association's first decade, with the emphasis on public documents and on scientific topics. A meeting on 10 October 1895 combined presentations on "Bibliography at the Leyden Conference of Zoologists" and "Bibliography at the Denver Conference of Librarians." H. Carrington Bolton delivered a paper on "The Bibliographic Work of the Smithsonian Institution" on 31 March 1897. After a presentation on 3 March 1901 on "State and Local Bibliography," members debated "Subject Catalogs vs. Bibliographies." In later years, programs on bibliographic topics became less frequent and more general, as members shared information at meetings such as "Current Bibliographical Work in Washington" (8 March 1911) and "National and International Bibliographical Projects" (10 November 1913).

PRINTING HISTORY AND SPECIAL COLLECTIONS

During DCLA's first decades, several papers were presented on the "literature" of a subject (e.g., "tobacco" on 8 March 1899 and "alchemy" on 11 April 1900), and reports were presented on events and meetings such as the New York Printing Exposition (9 May 1900) and the Bibliographical Society of America (14 March 1906). Well-known authorities also occasionally presented lectures (e.g., Wilberforce Eames on "Early Americana"—14 November 1900; William Dana Orcutt on "Printing as a Fine Art"—16 January 1908; and Herman H. B. Meyer on "The Principles of Good Book-Making"—18 February 1914). Illustrator and collector Joseph Pennell discussed "Illustrators: Past and Present" at a meeting on 20 January 1919.

Presentations and discussion about historical topics and special collections became less frequent after World War I. When such programs were deemed necessary, DCLA program planners knew they could rely on curators at the Library of Congress to talk about their collections. For example, Oscar Sonneck of the Music Division presented programs on 11 February 1903 ("The Musical Side of Benjamin Franklin") and 9 February 1916 (opera); Walter T. Swingle discussed the Chinese collection (17 November 1909 and 13 December 1916); A. V. Babine talked about Russian libraries and the Library of Congress's Russian collection (26 January 1910); Gaillard Hunt presented a paper about the Manuscript Division on 8 October 1913; Frederick W. Ashley discussed "Incunabula in the John Boyd Thatcher collection" on 17 February 1915 and the newly-acquired Vollbehr collection of incunabula on 5 February 1931; Arthur Hummel's presentation on 7 February 1928 was on "The Cultural Renaissance in China;" Samuel F. Bemis described his project of collecting documents about U.S. history in European archives at the 24 October 1929 meeting; and folklorist Alan Lomax spoke at a joint dinner meeting with the Baltimore chapter of the Special Libraries Association on 21 January 1939.

CATALOGING AND CLASSIFICATION

The first of many programs on aspects of cataloging and classification was held on 27 January 1897, with presentations by William P. Cutter on "Printed Card Indexes and Catalogs" and Albert B. Adams on "The Combining System of Notation in Classification." Between 1897 and 1901, the Library of Congress established its own classification system and card catalogs and began distributing printed catalog cards, enabling DCLA to feature "inside story" presentations on these and related topics by luminaries such as cataloging chief J. C. M. Hanson (9 March 1898), head classifier Charles Martel (11 January 1899 and 14 March 1900) and Librarian of Congress Herbert Putnam (12 December 1901).

The discussion topic for the 9 March 1904 program was nothing less than "Shall a numbered series of separate monographs on different subjects be classified individually or shelved as a set?" In 1922, in response to Margaret Mann, the chair of a committee to reorganize the Cataloging Section of the American Library Association, DCLA organized a Catalogers Group—apparently the first "special interest group" formed within the association. After its creation, few general program meetings were held on technical subjects. An exception was the 26 February 1937 presentation by Edwin Eliott Willoughby, chief bibliographer of the Folger Shakespeare Library, on "Cataloging the Folger Collection."

## WRITERS AND READERS

A discussion about "recent successful American writers" was held at the meeting of 9 May 1900, and Henrik Ibsen was the subject of a presentation on 12 February 1902. Two enormously successful public lectures about Shakespeare and Dante were sponsored in the lecture room of the new Public Library shortly after it opened. On 5 May 1903, more than three hundred people heard Sidney Smith speak on "Shakespeare, His Life and Works," and Theodore W. Koch topped that number on 10 February 1904, when an audience of 450 heard him lecture on "Dante, the Man and his Work." Then, except for two programs in 1909, "The Library of Robert Louis Stevenson" (13 January) and "Lyric Influences in the Poets' Corner of the Library of Congress" (14 April), literary topics practically disappeared from DCLA programs.

On 14 February 1912 at the Public Library, George Bowerman led a discussion on the "selection of books for public libraries." Years later he made presentations on "the outstanding books of 1924" (29 April 1925), and "best-sellers" (28 March 1934). If he was in town, it is likely that he participated in "A Symposium of Book Reviews," a special program on 24 February 1926, but the speakers' names are not recorded in the archives.

On 12 January 1938, a program at the National Archives about Works Progress Administration (WPA) arts projects featured Luther H. Evans, director of the Historical Records Survey, and Harry G. Alsberg, director of the Writers' Project. Perhaps inspired by the appointment of writer Archibald MacLeish as Librarian of Congress in 1939, a panel discussion on "cooperation between authors and librarians" was held on 26 March 1940. On 5 February 1941, Ralph Shaw, librarian at the Department of Agriculture, presented a program based on the recent book *What Reading Does to People*, by Douglas Waples, Bernard Berelson, and Franklyn R. Bradshaw. On 21 November 1944, Rudolph Flesch presented a program at the Library of Congress on "Getting Books and People Together."

In addition to sharing information about District of Columbia libraries and their collections through presentations, visits, and publications, DCLA members learned a great deal about other libraries, both in the United States and abroad. Libraries in the southern and western states were described in programs in 1898, 1902, 1905, and 1909 ("The New County Library System of California"). On 15 March 1905, director John Shaw Billings of the New York Public Library discussed his institution and its new building, which had been under construction for four years. Harvard librarian William C. Lane presented a program about his library on 12 December 1906.

Washington's growing importance as a diplomatic and international center was reflected in the relatively large number of programs about foreign libraries. The first was a talk on "The National Library of France" on 29 January 1896. Subsequent presentations often were "trip reports" on visits to libraries in Europe from prominent DCLA members such as Adler, Bowerman, Cutter, and Spofford, but others dealt with topics such as libraries in Australia, Russia, Puerto Rico, and South America, and the history of public libraries in Manchester, England. On 27 November 1926, former Princeton librarian Ernest C. Richardson tackled the ambitious topic of "International Cooperation and Local Problems."

During World War II, the horizons of DCLA members extended in many directions. The first joint meeting with the Inter-American Bibliographical Association on 20 February 1943, focused on libraries in South and Central America. On 12 October 1943, the American library in London was discussed and Harry M. Lydenberg, former director of the New York Public Library, described his plans as the new director of the Benjamin Franklin Library, the new U.S. government library in Mexico City. "The Effect of the War on British Libraries, Especially the British Museum" was discussed by British Museum officials on 17 January 1945 at a meeting at the Library of Congress cosponsored with the Washington, D.C. Chapter of the Special Libraries Association. The director of the Royal Library at The Hague and Dutch publisher Wouter Nijhoff made a presentation on 5 November 1945, on "Dutch Libraries, Publishing, and the Book Trade During the German Occupation and Afterwards."

## Technology

Not much was said about technology at DCLA programs between 1894 and 1945. The new bookbinding machinery at the Government Printing Office was described on 29 January 1896. A paper on 8 March 1899 about "A catalogue card sorting device" has not survived. On 10 December 1902, Spofford presented a paper on "The Mental and the Mechanical in Libraries," in which he displayed a healthy skepticism about "the great mass of improved machinery in our libraries," referring primarily to "pneumatic and electric book-carriers, and other time-saving devices." At the 30 January 1930 meeting, a U.S. Navy captain discussed "a new photographic aid in library research." The aid, as described by Isabel DuBois, the Bureau of Navigation librarian, in the April 1930 issue of the association's quarterly *D.C. Libraries* (1929-1970), was a "small kodak and projector" that a library could use "to replace or supplement the photostat in interlibrary loan." On 13 October 1938, the president of the American Documentation Institute presented a program on "Microfilm Reproduction of Printed Material" at a meeting held at the National Archives.

## DCLA AND WORLD WAR I

Shortly after America's entry into World War I in 1917, the American Library Association, in its first international project, assumed responsibility for furnishing library service to the American armed forces. Librarian of Congress Herbert Putnam became project director and DCLA, in spite of its weakened condition at the time, was supportive. At its 17 July 1917 meeting, an excursion to Great Falls to discuss the organization's plans for revival through reorganization, a contribution of $100 to the ALA's Library War Fund was approved. George Utley of the ALA described "Camp Libraries" at the 2 November meeting. On 22 January 1918, Congressman C. C. Dill of Washington state reported on his recent visit to the battlefields of France and Belgium. At the same meeting, a committee was established to cooperate with ALA in a book drive for servicemen and, by May, more than fifty-seven thousand books and $100 in cash had been gathered. "The Rehabilitation of Blind Soldiers" and "The Human Side of Camp Work" were the topics addressed at the DCLA program meeting on 18 March 1922, and members took an excursion to inspect the camp library at Camp Meade on 22 June 1918.

## EDUCATION FOR LIBRARIANSHIP

Training for librarians in the District of Columbia was a subject of continuing interest. At the 24 February 1897 meeting, Mary Fuller of the Department of the Interior Library proposed the resolution: "That this association take steps towards the establishment in this city of a library school." And indeed, a two-year course was established that year at Columbian University. All the faculty members were DCLA leaders: Ainsworth Rand Spofford held the position of director, and courses were given by H. Carrington Bolton, William Cutter, and Henderson Presnell. The curriculum, however, was never fully accredited by the American Library Association.

In 1923, a DCLA Committee on Library Training published *Washington's Facilities for Training in Library Science*, a twelve-page report that described courses at George Washington University, the Department of Agriculture, the Washington School for Secretaries, and Howard University. The report stimulated interest in improving library education and creating a graduate program in librarianship. The subject was discussed at a program meeting on 7 December 1923, and, on 7 December 1924, Herman H. B. Meyer presented a paper on "A Washington Graduate School of Library Science." The first graduate program in the

The need to provide books and library service to American soldiers unified librarians during World War I. The major effort, the American Library Association Library War Service, was supported by DCLA and headed by Librarian of Congress Herbert Putnam (standing in the center of an ALA photo taken on 5 January 1918). Its headquarters were at the Library of Congress in its first floor northwest pavilion.

area was not established until 1939 at Catholic University.

## SERVING THE PUBLIC

"Making the Library Useful," a lecture by Edward J. Farquhar on 14 March 1900, was the first DCLA program to focus on serving the public. Up until World War I, many of these programs were historical (e.g., "The Beginnings of Tax-Supported Public Libraries" on 8 February 1905 and "The Municipal Popular Libraries of Paris" on 23 October 1907) or specifically about the local situation (e.g., "Public Library Work in the District of Columbia" on 15 December 1909 and "Library Conditions in Maryland" on 22 March 1910). Tools available to librarians who serve the public were discussed on 20 April 1910 ("The Telephone in Library Work: Its Use and Misuse"), on 15 February 1911 ("The Bookmobile—Education on Wheels"), on 23 March 1923 ("What the Statistician Requires of the Librarian"), and on 25 April 1928, when Joseph L. Wheeler of the Enoch Pratt Free Library in Baltimore spoke on "Publicity as an Aid in the Work of Libraries."

Relationships between libraries and schools were discussed at programs on 8 April 1913 and on 20 October 1922, when the topic at a meeting at the Dodge Hotel Tea House was "Keeping Knowledge on Tap: Relations of the Public Schools and Libraries." The library and the community was a popular topic in the 1920s and 1930s (e.g., "The Life of a City Librar-ian" on 1 December 1922; "Opportunities of Librarians to Serve the Community" on 23 March 1923; "Local Social Problems and District Libraries" on 22 May 1924; and "The Relation of the Public Library to the Depression" on 29 March 1933).

Films were used in at least three programs in the association's first half century: on 15 December 1915 ("The Manufacture and Circulation of a Metropolitan Magazine"); on 30 January 1930 ("Teaching Students the Use of the Library"); and on 30 March 1941 when a film about the Montclair, NJ, Public Library was presented.

"The Public Library in 1974" was the title of a lively and creative skit presented by the Dramatic Club of the D.C. Public Library at the fortieth anniversary meeting on 24 October 1934. The action, taking place at a busy information desk forty years in the future, predicted astounding changes:

A job applicant, who satisfied the requirements of being able to spell in Esperanto and "work television, teletypewriter, telephoto, and photostat machines," was asked to report to work the next day when "we're broadvisioning World War Three."

The Library of Congress, which could be reached by "the Pa. Ave. subway or Air Taxie," had become the International Library and was supported by Congress "on a 60–40 basis—60 percent from member countries and 40 percent from the District of Columbia."

A group of children wanted to use the auditorium "to discuss the subject of problem parents."

At a retirement luncheon in 1940 to honor Dr. George F. Bowerman, director of the D.C. Public Library from 1904–1940 (and seen in the background), Librarian of Congress Archibald MacLeish congratulates Bowerman's successor, Clara W. Herbert. From 1925–1927, Miss Herbert was the first woman to serve as DCLA president.

## DCLA and World War II

The challenges presented by World War II to America and America's librarians were described to DCLA members by Librarian of Congress Archibald MacLeish at receptions on 15 December 1939 and on 24 October 1940. MacLeish's 1939 remarks, titled "The Obligations of Libraries in a Democracy," urged librarians to take a more active role in the political process, a message that many DCLA members took to heart. MacLeish's talk concluded:

> I do not believe libraries, any more than any other institution created by men, can be set above change; that librarianship, like every other human activity, must be continuously reinvented if it is to live; and that none, or so it seems to me, are under heavier responsibilities to the present than those whose profession is to conserve the past.

On 12 November 1941, in a program euphemistically titled "Aspects of Bibliography," the president of the British Library Association described how British libraries functioned under wartime conditions. The Japanese attack on Pearl Harbor, on 7 December 1941, stimulated programs about the role of books, reading, and libraries in wartime that continued through early 1945. The presentations began on 15 January 1942 with four talks on "Library War Work," and continued with programs on topics such as "The Victory Book Campaign" by Helen Keller and Mrs. Philip Sidney Smith (26 January 1942); "The Axis' New Order" (26 September 1942); "War Documentation" (20 February 1943); "Librarians and the War

Effort" (22 May 1943); and, on 20 February 1945, in a joint meeting with the Washington, D.C. Chapter of the Special Libraries Association, a session on "Librarians in Uniform" that included a discussion of "Reading Tastes in the Armed Forces."

## The Celebrations of the 1930s and 1940s

DCLA membership grew in the 1930s, exceeding 400 for the first time, and a self-congratulatory mood developed as the association approached its fortieth birthday in 1934. The anniversary celebration dinner, held at the Lafayette Hotel on 24 October 1934, set the tone for several dinners in the 1930s and 1940s at which the association celebrated itself and its most prominent members. Poetic tributes often enlivened these occasions, along with reminiscences from colleagues and light-hearted, self-deprecating humor. For example, at the 17 December 1936 dinner at the National Press Club honoring "Dr. and Mrs. F. W. Ashley," two lengthy odes were composed and read as tributes to the popular Frederick Ashley, a former DCLA president (1927–1929), who was retiring from a long career at the Library of Congress. The menu read:

Table of (your) Contents.
*Incipit: grapefruit cocktail a la Gutenberg.*
*Marginalia: celery and olives.*
*Gothic alphabet soup.*
*(Erratum–this will not be served).*
*Istanbul full levant duodeciom, rubrics in Cranberry sauce.*
*New peas, edition de poche (Covers wanting).*

*Sweet potatoes, enlarged and revised.  Auserwaehlt.*
*Brillat-Savarin hearts of lettuce, supplement Dostoievskii.*
*Revolt in the Dessert:- Arctica and Antarctica.*
*Colophon: At the sign of the Mocha and Java*

Helen T. Steinbarger of the D.C. Public Library was DCLA president when the association reached the half century mark in 1944.  Her invitation to the celebration on 24 October 1944—fifty years to the day from the first regular meeting at Columbia University—is an apt summary of fifty years of library growth in the Nation's capital:

During these fifty momentous years, the Library of Congress and its annex have been built, the National Archives established, and the Public Library system developed.  The "old line" departments have expanded into many new divisions and the "New Deal" and war periods have been marked by the establishment of many new departments, commissions and bureaus, each with a library or libraries.  Industrial, business, and labor organizations have added libraries.  The membership of the District of Columbia Library Association forms a truly cosmopolitan group.

# CHAPTER FIVE

# Publications

DCLA was established largely because of the concentration of library activity in Washington and the keen interest of librarians in forwarding their profession throughout the city. The desire of early members to learn about each other's libraries stimulated the preparation of the first DCLA publication, *Handbook; with Notes on Libraries in Washington*, which appeared in 1897 and described sixty-one libraries in the area. Supplements appeared in 1898 and 1900, and a new edition in 1904.

The next edition was ready in 1910, but no funds were available for publication. An appeal was made to the Library of Congress and an updated version was indeed published in 1914 in cooperation with the Library of Congress under the title, *Handbook of the Libraries in the District of Columbia*. It appeared just in time for the American Library Association's Washington convention, thanks largely to the initiative of its editor, Herman H. B. Meyer, chief bibliographer at the Library of Congress—who also happened to be DCLA's president in 1914–1915.

This 1914 *Handbook*, which described the holdings and activities of 137 libraries, and *Handbook of Washington's Informational Resources*, edited by Dorsey W. Hyde, Jr. and Miles O. Price and published in 1928, just in time for the Special Library Association's Washington convention, are the predecessors of the 1992 *Washington Area Library Directory* and other directories of library and information resources in the Washington area.

From 1922–1926, news of the association and the Washington library scene was reported in *DCLA Doings*, a single sheet issued on an occasional basis. At the 26 September 1929 meeting, Mary G. Lacy of the Bureau of Agricultural Economics proposed the idea of a periodical, whereupon she was immediately appointed chair of a committee to investigate the possibility. A month later she not only presented her report, but also distributed, in mimeographed form, Vol 1. No. 1 of *D.C. Libraries*, dated October 1929. The rationale behind its publication is clearly stated, along with an appeal:

The District of Columbia has the highest per capita average of book resources among the eleven great

## Handbook of Washington's Informational Resources

DORSEY W. HYDE, JR.

and

MILES O. PRICE
*Editors*

DISTRICT OF COLUMBIA LIBRARY ASSOCIATION
WASHINGTON, D. C.
1928

*Handbook of Washington's Informational Resources* was published by DCLA in 1928, just in time for the Special Library Association's Washington convention.

Publication of directories describing the incomparable library resources of the area has been an important DCLA accomplishment. Here is the most recent example.

cities of the world. . .IN VIEW OF THIS PROUD EMINENCE DO WE NOT NEED A LIBRARY ORGAN AS A MEANS OF ACHIEVING MORE COHERENCE AND UNITY AMONG THE LIBRARIANS OF THE DISTRICT OF COLUMBIA WHO ARE THE CUSTODIANS OF THIS TREASURE?

Thus prompted, through a ballot produced in the issue by the energetic Miss Lacy, members were asked if they thought the publication should be contin-

ued. Only forty-one out of approximately 400 ballots were returned but, not surprisingly, all were favorable. Thus DCLA's quarterly publication was established with Mary G. Lacy as editor, a job she held until 1933.

*D.C. Libraries*, which was published until 1970, went through several transformations. In the 1930s and 1940s, the emphasis was on membership and social news (including births, marriages, and

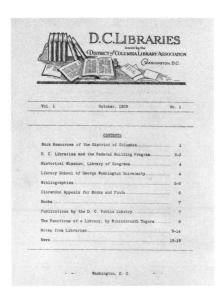

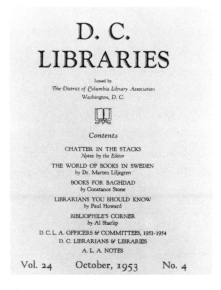

The publication of the periodical *D.C. Libraries* from 1929–1970 was by itself a major DCLA achievement. Through the years, its format and content reflected changes in both the tastes and the interests of DCLA members.

deaths), with brief reports about local libraries and association meetings and activities. DCLA officers in the 1950s felt that the publication deserved "a format more in keeping with the dignity of the organization and its ideals" and which would be more "distinguished" in appearance. Thus, in 1953, it became a "semi-scholarly" journal that was printed in a letterpress edition and accepted advertising. In the 1960s, however, the publication absorbed more and more of

DCLA's budget and, in 1970, the association's Executive Board ended its publication, along with that of *Clips & Quotes*, an occasional newsletter. The Board's reason was "we had neither editors nor money in the treasury to support both publications. Also, it was felt that neither publication was really meeting the needs of DCLA's membership." The two publications were replaced by *Intercom*, which focused on news about association activities.

# CHAPTER SIX

*◈◈◈*

# DCLA and Other Library Associations

THE cooperative relationship that exists today between DCLA and the American Library Association started slowly, primarily because of the local nature of many of the early DCLA projects. The situation began to change as DCLA neared the end of its second decade, and on 13 October 1913, George P. Utley, ALA's executive secretary, presented a program on "The Work of the ALA." DCLA's participation in ALA's World War I projects to provide books to the armed forces brought the two organizations closer together.

Two DCLA program meetings in 1920 were dedicated to "The Enlarged Program of the ALA," a plan for greatly expanded ALA activity. The "Enlarged Program" proved to be too ambitious for ALA, but its failure emphasized the need for additional ALA members—both individual and organizational. One of the consequences was that DCLA, on 28 June 1922, officially became an ALA "chapter" and began sending a representative to ALA meetings. The new relationship began on a positive note when, in 1923, DCLA became the first local chapter to contribute (the sum

was $25) to the ALA fund for a new headquarters building. In October 1926, DCLA hosted foreign librarians who were on their way to Chicago to celebrate ALA's fiftieth anniversary; one of the events was a reception at the Mayflower Hotel where President Calvin Coolidge greeted the delegates. By 1937, DCLA members were heavily involved in ALA activities, with not less than thirty-six Washington librarians serving on various ALA committees.

Through the years the relationship has been strengthened by common interests such as library legislation and through individuals who have led both organizations. Six librarians have served as president of both DCLA and ALA: Herbert Putnam (DCLA 1920–1922, ALA 1898, 1903–1904); William Warner Bishop (DCLA 1910–1911, ALA 1918–1919); Herman H. B. Meyer (DCLA 1914–1915, ALA 1924–1925); Lucile M. Morsch (DCLA 1954–1955, ALA 1957–1958); Elizabeth W. Stone (DCLA 1966–1967, ALA 1981–1982); and Hardy R. Franklin (DCLA 1992–1993, ALA 1993–1994).

Regional cooperation among library organizations has been a DCLA concern since 1897, when the possibility of a combined District of Columbia-Maryland library association was discussed. A joint meeting of the Washington, New Jersey, and Pennsylvania library associations was held on 29–31 March 1900. In 1915, prompted by declining membership rolls, DCLA commissioned a feasibility study for a tri-state (District of Columbia-Maryland-Virginia) library association. A joint meeting of the three associations was held in Annapolis on 17 October 1925, and, on 19 February 1928, it was agreed that DCLA would become a member of a new regional association.

The first meeting of the new Columbian Library Association was held at the Dodge Hotel Tea House on 19 January 1929. This organization, which in 1933 changed its name to the Middle Eastern Library Association, was dominated by DCLA and the Maryland Library Association. It met annually until 1939 when representatives of the library associations of Pennsylvania, New Jersey, and Delaware joined the group. The old Middle Eastern Library Association was abolished in 1940. Regional activity slowed during World War II, but was formally reestablished in 1949, under the auspices of the ALA, when the Middle Atlantic States Regional Federation was created.

DCLA and local chapters of the Special Library Association (SLA) began a history of cordial relations in January 1939 when DCLA held a joint meeting with the Baltimore SLA chapter. In the 1940s, DCLA and the new Washington, D.C. Chapter of SLA (established 1940) began coordinating their program schedules and sponsoring joint meetings, including presentations about the effect of World War II on libraries and librarianship and, on 12 August 1948, a program featuring F. R. Ranganathan, president of the Indian Library Association and Abdul Noneim Omar, director of the Egyptian National Library. Social events also were cosponsored, such as a dinner and reception at the Statler Hotel for Clara W. Herbert on 12 December 1946 on the occasion of her retirement from the D.C. Public Library. Another joint event was a book auction, held 16 December 1952 at the Pan American Union. The auctioneer was Chief Assistant Librarian of Congress Verner W. Clapp, who for many years also served as DCLA's official representative to the American Library Association.

꧁꧂

# CHAPTER SEVEN

# Federal Libraries and Librarians

DCLA's members have always had a strong interest in issues relating to government libraries—which is hardly surprising since historically 65–70 percent of its members have been federal librarians. The percentage of government librarians, particularly from the Library of Congress, was even higher in the association's first decade. Thirty-four of the 44 charter members were federal librarians (5 of the 34 were from the Library of Congress) and in 1898, when membership reached 102, sixty were federal librarians and one-third of their number were Library of Congress employees.

The Library of Congress began to play an even more prominent role among federal libraries and within DCLA in 1899 after Herbert Putnam became Librarian of Congress. Putnam encouraged professional activity and DCLA soon began serving as the major professional association for Library of Congress officials and staff members—a role it continued to play into the 1960s. In 1902, when DCLA's membership had reached 181, no fewer than 77 were from the Library of Congress. During the crisis of 1914–1917, when the future of the organization was in doubt, the willingness

of Library of Congress officers Herman H. B. Meyer and William Slade to serve two terms each as DCLA president helped keep the association together.

However, it was not a Library of Congress employee but George F. Bowerman, director of the D.C. Public Library, who took the lead in an area where DCLA eventually made perhaps its single most important contribution to the library profession: the reclassification of federal library jobs and salaries.

At the end of World War I, Congress established a Joint Commission on Reclassification to reclassify positions in government service. Bowerman wrote DCLA president Theodore W. Koch, on 19 January 1919, urging DCLA to bring the status and relatively low salaries of government librarians to the commission's attention. Bowerman said he also would press the case with the ALA, since the status of librarians in the nation's capital affected the status of librarians across the country; he wrote an article on the topic for the May 1919 issue of the *ALA Bulletin*. A skilled witness before Congressional committees and an astute lobbyist, Bowerman, through the Retirement Act of

Herbert Putnam, Librarian of Congress (1899–1939) and DCLA president (1920–1921), encouraged library use by everyone. Less than a year after the new Library of Congress building opened, the hours were expanded to allow the public to use it on weekends and in the evening. Here Putnam is pictured among students in the Library's Main Reading Room.

1920, managed to bring D.C. Public Library staff members into the federal employees' retirement system.

Both DCLA and ALA established committees. In fact DCLA eventually created three different committees: one on reclassification, one on "defining library positions," and, perhaps in anticipation of unsatisfactory results, a committee on legislation. The need to reclassify and upgrade government library positions was discussed at DCLA meetings on 23 October 1919; 24 March and 29 October 1920; 26 May 1922; and 1 December 1922, when Senator Thomas Stirling from South Dakota made so many favorable promises and statements that his address was published in the journal *Public Libraries*.

The Classification Act was finally approved in 1923, but DCLA members were dismayed when the classification board established by the new law immediately classified most federal librarians (excepting only a few Library of Congress division chiefs and the librarians of the Bureau of Entomology and of the Patent Office) as clerical workers and put them in grades where their current salaries were frozen.

A new twelve-person DCLA committee, chaired by Dorsey W. Hyde, Jr., quickly prepared and published a ninety-four-page document, *Brief and Specifications for Library Service in the Federal Government*, which again made the case, this time through concrete examples, for librarians to be recognized as professionals. DCLA strongly endorsed the report at its meeting on 2 November 1923, and soon the chairman of the Personnel Classification Board reluctantly agreed to assign a "trained investigator," a Mr.

George F. Bowerman, director of the D.C. Public Library from 1904–1940, is depicted in a painting by Richard S. Meryman, a Washington artist. A major influence in DCLA, Bowerman served as president in 1906–1907 and led the successful movement between 1919-1923 to reclassify federal librarians.

Bowman, to restudy the issue. The outcome is described in a letter from Miles O. Price, DCLA president in 1924–1925, to Rev. James J. Kortendick, president of DCLA from 1952–1954:

> The final result of our year's work with Mr. Bowman was that librarians were to be recognized in our report as professionals, and the grading was to be done on a job basis, not the basis of existing salaries. The report, on a bleak Friday afternoon, one day away from the deadline, was profanely rejected *in toto* by the P.C.B. Chairman (Mr. Bailey), with the order to go out and bring something back that made sense.

Sink or swim—Mr. Bowman by this time was a firm convert—the original report was brought back the next day intact, except for a page boy (position) in the D.C. Public Library; whereupon Mr. Bailey smiled graciously and said, "O.K., if that's what you really believe," and our fight was won.

Librarians as a large group were, for the first time in America, recognized as professionals. The average salary increase over the original allocations was a whopping one-third.

The need to promote cooperation among federal libraries has been a theme throughout DCLA's history, even though it has not been the organization's principal purpose. The idea became part of the public agenda for libraries during the New Deal of the 1930s, a time of government growth and increased federal activity. A "national plan for libraries," approved by the American Library Association in 1934, called for a federal library agency. The next year, ALA published a report titled A *Federal Library Agency and Federal Library Aid*, which concluded that a single federal agency was needed "to give leadership to a coordination of Federal library activities;" in 1936, DCLA approved a resolution calling for the creation of such an agency in the Department of Education.

In 1938, a library office was established in the Department of Education, but the mission of the new Library Services Division was narrower than the one conceived for the federal library agency. It was a good start, however. The author of an article in *D.C. Libraries* about the new office felt "this beginning of a federal activity toward libraries augurs well for the future, and needs only the whole-hearted cooperation of librarians, library associations and friends of libraries everywhere" to develop "real library leadership in the National Capital." Under the effective leadership of Ralph Dunbar, the division gathered library statistics, carried out studies and surveys, and promoted library development.

Interestingly, three years earlier, when asked by ALA officials if the Library of Congress might become the home of a "national" library agency, Librarian of Congress Herbert Putnam refused to even consider the question, stating that such activities "would tend to confuse and impede the service to learning, which should be the primary duty of our National Library."

In 1937, an ALA Special Committee on Federal Relations, chaired by Carleton B. Joeckel, recommended that "a Federal Library Council" be established "to coordinate the policies and procedures of the libraries of the Federal Government." From 1938 to 1940, a DCLA Committee on Federal Libraries supported the idea, which was officially endorsed by DCLA members at their meeting on 26 April 1939. The committee continued its work, reporting in 1940 that its chief objective during the year had been the creation of the council to help, it awkwardly explained, "in those Federal library problems which it would seem only joint action, as opposed to individual effort, can solve."

While no federal council was officially created, from 1941 to 1948, DCLA members participated in meetings of a group which called itself the "Informal Federal Librarians' Council" and met to discuss familiar topics such as civil service classification, duplication of collections, interlibrary loan, and the procurement of foreign publications.

The idea of an advisory group "seeking to improve the operations of Federal libraries" was reintroduced in a 1963 *Report on Federal Departmental Libraries* sponsored by the Brookings Institution, with funding from the Council on Library Resources. The report was based on a survey of federal libraries that took place from July 1959 through June 1961. The project was headed by former Librarian of Congress (1945–1953) Luther H. Evans; Ralph Dunbar served as research associate. The effort was endorsed by DCLA, the Washington, D.C. Chapter of the Special Libraries Association, and the Law Librarians' Society of Washington, D.C. Director Evans described the project and presented a condensed version of the questionnaire in the January 1960 issue of *D.C. Libraries*.

In addition to gathering information, the study identified specific issues and problems facing federal libraries (e.g., procurement, automation, and standards). The Brookings Institution convened a "conference of experts" in 1963 to consider the report and the federal library council idea. The conference endorsed the recommendation in the following form: "That the Library of Congress and the Bureau of the Budget jointly invite appropriate agencies to explore the desirability of establishing a continuing interagency group to advise on the problems of federal libraries."

The story finally reached a happy conclusion

Paul Howard, president of DCLA 1947–1948, helped establish the Federal Library Committee and served as its first executive director. He also was the first director of ALA's Washington office.

when the Bureau of the Budget and the Library of Congress, on 23 March 1965, formed the Federal Library Committee. With alacrity, in fact six days before the committee was officially established, DCLA held a symposium at the Library of Congress on "The Establishment of the Federal Library Committee." The three papers presented at the meeting were published in the Summer 1965 issue of *D.C. Libraries*. One of the participants pointed to a last-minute change that those familiar with the federal bureaucracy would especially appreciate:

> In the earlier phases of our work, the name "Federal Library Council" was used, but with the publication of Budget Circular A-63, which prohibits the use of "Council" or "Commission" except for bodies established by Executive Order or by statute, the body was designated "Federal Library Committee."

The first executive director of the Federal Library Committee, Paul Howard, the former head of ALA's Washington office and the Department of the Interior Library, reported on the committee's "progress and prospects" in the Winter 1969 issue of *D.C. Libraries*.

In 1969, through a resolution to President Nixon and the work of its legislative committee, DCLA also actively supported another major development on the federal library scene: the formation of a permanent National Commission on Libraries that would develop national library policy and "strengthen the role of libraries in our society." The National Commission on Libraries and Information Science was established in July 1970.

In 1984, the Federal Library Committee was renamed the Federal Library and Information Center Committee (FLICC). As the federal interagency advisory committee that provides leadership and assistance to the nation's 2,500 federal libraries and information centers, it promotes services, coordinates resources, provides professional training, and recommends policies, programs, and procedures. Through the Federal Library and Information Network (FEDLINK), a cooperative program established in the mid-1970s, FLICC offers contractual services to all federal agencies.

# CHAPTER EIGHT

## Library Issues and Legislative Action

BEING located in the library and information center *and* in the political center of the country has made it easy for DCLA members—and particularly DCLA officers—to become involved in legislative matters regarding libraries. This interest in legislation and politics has been evident since DCLA's early days. For example, on 27 May 1896, Henderson Presnell of the Bureau of Education Library delivered a paper on the history of library legislation in the United States. A contemporary perspective was offered on 14 November 1900, when Smithsonian librarian Cyrus Adler spoke on "Legislation Affecting Library Interests Before the Last Congress." Other examples, all mentioned previously, include DCLA's catalytic role in the creation by Congress of the D.C. Public Library, the work of DCLA's legislative committee in the reclassification struggle of 1919–1923, and the efforts of its committee on federal libraries in the campaign for a federal library council.

Since the 1930s, DCLA has generally followed the lead of the American Library Association regarding library legislation at the national level, supporting ALA initiatives and, because of its strategic

Washington location, hosting many events of social and potential political significance. For example, on 3 March 1936, the association—still keenly interested in job classification for professional librarians—held a dinner at the Lafayette Hotel honoring the three U.S. Civil Service commissioners. One hundred and fifty people attended. The librarians present praised the "fairness" of the commissioners who, in turn, told of the help and influence of individual librarians whom they had known and admired through the years.

Although federal aid to libraries did not become a reality until the mid-1950s, the leaders of the American Library Association began talking about the possibility decades earlier. However, many librarians were themselves opposed to the notion, regarding the support of education and libraries strictly as a state and local responsibility. At the annual ALA conference in Denver in 1935, three state library associations—Connecticut, Massachusetts, and New Jersey—even presented resolutions against federal aid to libraries.

The DCLA annual banquet on 1 April 1936 was, therefore, very good news for ALA officials and other proponents of a stronger federal role on behalf of

## What Libraries Mean to the Nation

BY ELEANOR ROOSEVELT

*An Address given at the*
*District of Columbia Library Association Dinner*
*Carlton Hotel, Washington, D. C.*
*April 1, 1936*

DISTRICT OF COLUMBIA LIBRARY
ASSOCIATION

**DINNER**

WEDNESDAY, APRIL 1, 1936
8:00 P. M.

CARLTON HOTEL

135

$2.00

TABLE No. / 7

Eleanor Roosevelt's 1936 speech at the DCLA annual banquet (the text, published for DCLA by the American Library Association, and the ticket for the dinner are shown at top and bottom) gave the movement for federal aid to libraries a major boost.

libraries. The principal speaker, Mrs. Franklin D. Roosevelt, was to discuss "What Libraries Mean to the Nation." Moreover, the other speakers were Representative Kent Keller of Illinois, speaking on "Our National Library," and Senator William H. King of Utah, addressing the topic "The Library in Adult Education."

More than three hundred people attended the dinner, held at the Carlton Hotel, and they were not disappointed. Congressman Keller, who served on the Joint Committee on the Library, praised the Library of Congress and Senator King, a member of the Senate District of Columbia subcommittee, promised to help the D.C. Public Library obtain funds for a larger central library building. Eleanor Roosevelt's talk, characterized by the Washington *Evening Star* as "a plea for the democratization of culture," emphasized the need for libraries in rural and other hard-to-reach places throughout America. Moreover,

> Our libraries should be used to create a new life of the mind. Great changes in civilization are upon us, and what we do will depend on how much we know. Libraries are tremendously vital. They have a chance to help to make a democracy that will be a real democracy.

The talk was published for DCLA by the American Library Association; 15,000 copies were printed and distributed. DCLA relations with Mrs. Roosevelt remained good, and in May 1941 she hosted 600 association members at a White House garden party. Ten years later, Mrs. Roosevelt's theme of extending public library service to rural America was the focal point of the first bill for federal aid to libraries introduced in Congress.

In addition to the dinners with the Civil Service commissioners and Mrs. Roosevelt, a reception honoring Archibald MacLeish, President Roosevelt's choice to be Librarian of Congress, was held in cooperation with the Library of Congress staff on 15 December 1939 at the Department of the Interior; more than one thousand people attended. Mr. MacLeish hosted DCLA members at the Library of Congress on 24 October 1940.

A tradition had been established and Luther Evans, who in mid-1945 had been nominated by President Truman and confirmed by the Senate as Librarian of Congress, was honored at a DCLA reception on 26 October 1945. Mamie Eisenhower hosted DCLA officers at the White House on 14 January 1954, and President Eisenhower's selection as Librarian of Congress, L. Quincy Mumford, was honored on 2 October 1954 at a reception at the Pan American Union, an event cosponsored with the Special Libraries Association. Rosalyn Carter hosted the DCLA new members reception at the White House on 9 November 1978.

A more active form of political involvement for DCLA members and other librarians began in October 1945, when the American Library Association established a Washington office. Its purpose was to lobby for library legislation and to form closer relationships with the Office of Education, federal libraries, and the federal government in general. The director of the ALA Washington Office from 1945–1949

was Paul Howard, who also served as DCLA president in 1947–1948.

The Public Library Services Demonstration Bill was introduced in Congress in 1946. This first attempt to obtain federal aid for libraries was discussed, at a DCLA meeting on 19 February 1948, by Senator George D. Aiken of Vermont and the state librarian of Ohio. The bill was reintroduced in each session of Congress until 1950 when, to the surprise of many, it was defeated by a vote of 164–161. Paul Howard worked hard on behalf of the bill. However, in the midst of his efforts, ALA closed the Washington office because of lack of funds and Howard moved to the Department of the Interior as its librarian. At its 12 December 1949 meeting, DCLA members voted to contribute $100 toward the re-establishment of the Washington office.

ALA was able to make new financial arrangements and reopened its Washington office with a new director, Marjorie Malmberg, on 1 January 1950. A new effort for federal aid for libraries was mounted. The bill introduced in 1951, and reintroduced for the next five sessions of congress, was carefully tailored and the promotion and lobbying efforts on its behalf were skillfully planned. DCLA and its members naturally were part of the campaign. *D.C. Libraries* regularly published "notes" from the ALA Washington office that described the situation. Readers of the January 1953 issue, for example, were reminded by Julia D. Bennett of the ALA Washington office:

All librarians should be aware of this piece of Federal legislation, which, if passed, would assist tremendously

This bookmobile belonged to the city's Model Cities Project, in which the D.C. Public Library was a participant. Launched in 1970 as an outreach to the neglected and riot-damaged inner city, the Project's bookmobiles provided a visible, inviting, and effective grass-roots symbol of libraries and their importance until they fell victim to city-wide budget cuts.

Legislative activity on behalf of libraries became imperative with the advent of difficult times for library funding in the 1970s. DCLA formed a Legislative Committee in 1973 and, in 1975, a Legislative Day, when librarians formally visited legislators on Capitol Hill (*at left* is the cover of the 1981 program). Legislative Day soon became a national cooperative effort with the ALA Washington office, the Special Libraries Association and other library advocates. The 1992 delegation *at right* includes then DCLA president, Hardy R. Franklin.

in giving public library service to the approximately thirty million Americans now without such service. When you talk with Congressmen, Senators, and individuals in government positions, be sure to tell them about this bill and the need for its passage.

Julia Bennett, Paul Howard, and Robert Frase of the American Book Publishers Council were the featured speakers at a 23 April 1953 DCLA meeting on "Current Legislation Affecting Books and Libraries."

The new Library Services Bill was approved in 1956. The emphasis was still on rural areas and many supporters felt that the popularity and "sex appeal" of the bookmobile, the major means of reaching most rural areas, played an important role in its passage.

The federal commitment to libraries increased substantially between 1956 and 1968. The rural service program was extended to urban areas and new legislation included funds for the construction of libraries,

The Martin Luther King Memorial Library, headquarters of the D.C. Public Library System, nears completion. Designed by the internationally famous architect Mies van der Rohe, the building at 9th and G Streets, NW, opened in September 1972.

interlibrary cooperation, institutional library services at elementary and secondary schools and at colleges, and the expansion of the Library of Congress, the Armed Forces Medical Library (designated the National Library of Medicine in 1956), the Department of Agriculture Library (designated the National Agricultural Library in 1962), and other federal libraries.

The ALA Washington office played a crucial role in this "golden age" of governmental library support, and DCLA helped—as an organization and through the involvement of its individual members.

ALA office director Julia Bennett wrote a column about legislative and ALA topics in D.C. *Libraries* from 1955–1958, and her successor, Germaine Krettek, contributed occasional reports in subsequent years. Most of DCLA's political actions took the form of telegrams or letters of support for federal library legislation (1963, 1968); for school libraries in the District of Columbia (1960, 1964, 1965, 1968); and for the budget request of the D.C. Public Library (1966, 1968).

More difficult times for library funding at both the federal and local levels came in the 1970s, and legislative activity on behalf of libraries became more important than ever. Eileen D. Cooke, who had worked in ALA's Washington office since 1964, became its director in 1972 and her effective leadership quickly began to make a difference.

DCLA formally created a Legislative Committee in 1973 and, in 1975, organized a Legislative Day, when librarians visited legislators on Capitol Hill. Legislative Day soon became a national, cooperative effort sponsored with the ALA Washington office, the Special Libraries Association, and other library advocates. Today the ALA Washington office takes the lead in providing information and ideas for Library Legislative Day, which is held each April during National Library Week, but DCLA's Legislative Committee and membership continue to play a major role in organizing mailings, arranging for the reception, and providing needed staff support.

In the same vein, DCLA has played an active "local arrangements" role in the White House Conferences on Library and Information Services that were held in Washington, D.C., on 15–19 November 1979 and 9–13 July 1991.

Nor has DCLA neglected the local scene. In 1979, the association intensified its legislative activity on behalf of the D.C. Public Library, the library it had helped bring into existence in 1894–1898. In the 1970s, the D.C. library system's budget was cut every year except 1976, and even deeper cuts were threatened. In 1979, DCLA president Nancy E. Gwinn testified on behalf of the Public Library in its budget hearings before the D.C. City Council. She also named library activist Charmaine Yochim to head the association's Legislative Committee. The committee organized public rallies in 1979, 1980, and 1981 and, under Yochim's leadership, the committee and its members became involved in a wide range of activities on behalf of the city's publicly supported libraries.

A new community-wide coalition, the D.C. Citizen Advocates for Libraries (CAL) was formed in 1981. DCLA was part of the coalition, which also included Friends of Libraries Groups (many of them formed in the early 1980s), the D.C. Association of School Librarians, educational organizations, and interested citizens. CAL continued its effective work through 1986 when the mayor took a major step to restore the budgetary losses incurred during the previous decade. Support continues today through the Federation of Friends of the District of Columbia Public Library System.

# CHAPTER NINE

~SVS~

# DCLA and its Members in Today's World

LIKE most professional organizations, DCLA has gone through periods of enthusiasm and great activity and periods of decline and lethargy. To its credit, it also is prone to periods of self-examination, which means polling its members every few years. A 1922 questionnaire suggested the following subjects for committee activity: library cooperation, reclassification of positions, library training, employment, publicity, membership, and entertainment. The results were discussed at a "program of work" at the Dodge Hotel Tea House on 22 March 1922. Perhaps anticipating the worst, at the same meeting DCLA officers asked William L. Lewis to make a presentation on "The Need for Intelligent Thinking in the Postwar Years."

In April 1948, a committee chaired by Lucile M. Morsch mailed a questionnaire to 2,300 individuals as part of a "census of librarians" in the metropolitan Washington area. The purpose of the questionnaire was to enable DCLA "to serve the profession more effectively by determining who are the librarians, what are their problems, what are their interests," and concurrently, to enable Washington's librarians "to serve

their clientele more effectively through the knowledge of their own strengths and common interests." Unfortunately, nothing seems to have been done with the results—in fact, the results seem to have disappeared. However, the questions by themselves indicate DCLA's overall direction, for they suggest the creation of membership "groups"—by activity (e.g., technical processes), by subject (e.g., science and technology), and by type of library (e.g., legislative reference).

Reading discussion groups were another specialized area of increasing interest in the late 1940s and early 1950s. The growth of this "movement" at the D.C. Public Library in the 1950s was described in the article "Group Discussion and the Library" by John T. Cheney in the January 1954 issue of *D.C. Libraries.*

In 1954, the DCLA executive board decided that all programs should have a professional (not general) interest, and the 1957 executive board approved the idea of "interest groups" that would aid in the professional development of younger members. However, the notion of multiple specialized interest groups was not implemented until 1966.

In the mid-1960s, DCLA was revitalized and expanded under the energetic leadership of Elizabeth Stone, the dean of the School of Library Science at Catholic University and DCLA president in 1966–1967. She began her service by sending a questionnaire to members, but followed up by convening an "Idea Day" at which members discussed ways they wanted to be involved with the organization.

The result, as outlined in the DCLA annual report for 1966–1967, was the creation of not less than fifteen interest groups, divided into four general categories: intercommunication and hospitality; idea exchange and continuing education (e.g., children's and young adult librarians); promotion of specific kinds of library service (e.g., literacy, library service to the blind and physically handicapped); and long-range planning for the association. With fifteen interest groups and fifteen committees (ranging alphabetically from Archives to Publicity), participation soared and DCLA membership rose to an all-time high of 1,018.

Another result of "Idea Day" was the establishment of a pattern of meetings that still exists today. The traditions of an annual dinner meeting with a noted guest speaker and holding programs in different libraries were continued. However, the number of program meetings was cut, with one of those meetings established as a purely social affair and another an all-day workshop where one topic could be explored in depth.

The first such Spring Workshop, organized by Dr. Stone with help from Eileen Cooke and others, was held on 11 March 1967 at Catholic University;

Elizabeth W. Stone, Dean of the School of Library and Information Science, the Catholic University of America, revitalized DCLA during her term as president, 1966–1967.

the topic was "Problems of Automation and Manpower." The next year, the Washington, D.C. Chapter of the Special Libraries Association became the co-sponsor of what has become an annual Joint Spring Workshop; other organizations have also joined in the sponsorship. Each workshop is now viewed (and advertised) as a major "continuing education" opportu-

Eileen D. Cooke, director of the ALA Washington office, 1972–1994, and 1993–1994 ALA president Hardy R. Franklin.

nity for Washington area librarians. Management and technology topics have dominated; the 1991 workshop, for example, was on "Paperless Publishing and the Library: CD-ROM, Online and Beyond." In 1992, the topic was "Access and Availability: Making the Government's Information Public;" the 1993 program was on "Maximizing User Satisfaction," and the title of the 1994 workshop was "The Habit of Being: Toward Professional Effectiveness."

The 1966–1967 annual report contained a new statement of association objectives (labeled "tentative draft—no. 2") that proposed the following goals and obligations: (1) promotion of library service and librarianship; (2) active contribution to the profession of librarianship; (3) pursuit of benefits for association members; (4) establishment and maintenance of professional and cooperative relationships; and (5) achievement of a meaningful role of the library in society. A qualifying statement (in all probability inserted to appease an unhappy committee member!) concludes this assertion of new objectives: "It is recognized that the achievement of any purpose must be necessarily accompanied by continued review of the Association's goals and by maintaining an attitude of flexibility and vitality among its membership."

In 1966, the DCLA Board of Directors adopted an official emblem for the organization. It is a shield device, based on the George Washington family shield as adapted by James Thackara and John Vallance and first imprinted on a map of the City of Washington engraved in 1792.

DCLA celebrated its seventy-fifth anniversary in 1969. Author Alex Haley spoke at the anniversary dinner in May, and 250 people attended a special reception held in the Library of Congress's Whittall Pavilion on 29 October 1969. Dues increases were a hallmark of the past quarter century, edging up to $10 a year in 1970, to $15 in 1983, and reaching $20 in 1990. On 31 July 1979, DCLA received tax-exempt status under provisions of section 501 (c) (3) of the Internal Revenue Code.

By 1986, the number of DCLA committees and interest groups had been reduced considerably. The committees were Federal Legislation, Intellectual Freedom, and Legislative; the interest groups were

Children and Young Adults, Genealogy and Local History, Government Documents, Management, Reference, and Technical Services. Moreover, DCLA's statement of purpose had been modified to recognize the information age:

> to promote and support libraries and information centers and to provide for professional development, continuing education, and collegial exchange among librarians and information specialists in Washington, D.C. and vicinity.

A microcomputer interest group, established during the 1987–1988 presidency of Molly Raphael, eventually evolved into the Library Technology interest group.

The presence of two accredited graduate library schools in the area, Catholic University and the University of Maryland, has strengthened interest in library education. Under the leadership of president Shirley Loo, in 1990 DCLA established a Student Loan Fund to assist library school students through interest free loans and the Ainsworth Rand Spofford President's Award for outstanding contributions to the library community. In 1991, some DCLA members,

recognizing the regional nature of the association, suggested a name change (e.g., the Capital Area Library Association). There was immediate opposition and the question was tabled—at least through the centennial year!

However, the evolution of DCLA's committees and interests has continued. Today, in the centennial year, the committees are: Archives, Awards, Intellectual Freedom, Membership, National Library Legislative Day, Nominating, and Student Loan. There are eight interest groups: Children and Young Adults; Genealogy, Local History and Folklore; Government Documents; Intellectual Freedom; Library Technology; Management; Preservation; Reference; and Technical Services. Individuals with special functions include a federal relations liaison, the editor of the newsletter *Intercom*, a student representative, and representatives to the Middle Atlantic Region Library Federation. The Board of Directors consists of a president, a vice-president/president-elect, recording secretary, treasurer, membership secretary, immediate past president, three directors, and the chapter councilor to the American Library Association.

# CONCLUSION
❧

THE nature of DCLA as an organization has changed considerably since its establishment. It began as a "library club," more akin to other intellectual societies formed in Washington in the last decades of the nineteenth century than to a state library association—or what we today would call a "service-oriented" organization. Its initial tendency towards exclusiveness ended with the membership crisis of 1914–1917, which stretched into the 1920s. Until the 1950s, most of its officers were senior library officials, and often head librarians. Beginning in the 1950s, but especially in the mid-1960s, DCLA succeeded in opening itself up to younger professionals; many of them became officers or, more likely, active in one of the growing number of interest groups. DCLA's appeal today comes mostly from the opportunities it offers members for continuing education and career advancement in an era of increasing specialization.

Looking back over the record of a very full one hundred years, how might one characterize DCLA and the activities of its members? Phrases that come to mind include flexibility and willingness to change (albeit, often provoked by a crisis); exceptionally wide-ranging professional interests; seriousness of purpose; a particular pride (that often shows) in the library and information resources of the Nation's Capital; a special concern with federal libraries, even though the association—pursuing its stated intention of 1894—has successfully included librarians from many different kinds of libraries; a willingness to cooperate with other library associations and groups (for both success and survival); and, particularly among its leaders, a keen appreciation of the need to be involved in legislative issues and action.

While today many of the programs and workshops are concerned with new technologies, the theme of service—to those served by federal, public, college and university, and school librarians—is just as strong. In fact it was emphasized by Hardy R. Franklin, director of the D.C. Public Library and recent president of both the District of Columbia Library Association and the American Library Association, who developed program initiatives around his presidential theme: "Customer Service, The Heart of the Library."

In honor of the centennial of DCLA and National Library Week, a tree planting ceremony was held on 21 April 1993. A tree each was planted at two D.C. Public Library branches; this photo shows the planting at the Washington Highlands branch.

Today, after a century of promoting libraries and library service, DCLA remains a strong and unifying presence in the Washington, D.C., metropolitan area. Its 800 members participate in a constantly evolving and varied program of activities that began in the age of print and has carried the organization into the information age of the 1990s. DCLA's contribution to libraries and to the library and information profession is just as important as it was a century ago.

# SOURCES

⋯⋯

THIS brief volume is not a complete history of the District of Columbia Library Association. It includes the highlights of DCLA's history but omits detailed information about governance, committees, membership, and other administrative concerns.

A reasonably full record of DCLA and its activities exists in the association archives housed in the Washingtoniana Division in the Martin Luther King Memorial Library, the headquarters building of the D.C. Public Library System. The major categories of materials in the DCLA Archives are five bound volumes of minutes and clippings covering the years 1894–1954; executive board minutes, beginning in 1937; notebooks and manuals prepared for association officers, beginning in 1965; and publications, 1894–. There are many gaps in these holdings, but miscellaneous clippings and ephemera help round out the picture.

This book relies mostly on these archives, especially the first volume of minutes, 1894–1921; on DCLA publications (see Appendix II), particularly D.C. Libraries (1929–1970), and Intercom (1971–); and on an unpublished master's degree dissertation,

Martha Seabrook's "A History of the District of Columbia Library Association, 1894–1954," which was submitted in 1957 in partial fulfillment of the requirements for the degree of master of science in library science at Catholic University of America. These sources, cited below as DCLA Archives, DCLib, Intercom, and Seabrook, were supplemented by other publications, as indicated in the summary that follows.

## 1. WASHINGTON, D.C., IN THE 1880s AND 1890s

Background information was obtained from: Constance McLaughlin Green, Washington, Capital City, 1879–1950 (1963):76–100; Pamela Scott and Antoinette J. Lee, Buildings of the District of Columbia (1993), especially pp. 62–112; J. Kirkpatrick Flack, Desideratum in Washington: The Intellectual Community in the Capital City, 1870–1900 (1975); and Douglas E. Evelyn and Paul Dickson, On This Spot: Pinpointing the Past in Washington, D.C. (1992). The Carpenter quote is in Frank G. Carpenter, Carp's Washington, ed. by Frances Carpenter (1960): 93.

## 2. CREATING DCLA

In addition to the earliest records in the DCLA Archives and Seabrook, pp. 1–22, this chapter draws on the following brief histories of DCLA: Julia L. V. McCord, "History of the District of Columbia Library Association, 1894–1930," *DCLib* 1 (July 1930): 67–74; Adelaide R. Hasse, "A Backward Glance," *DCLib* 6 (Nov. 1934):2–5; David C. Mearns, "Many Happy Returns: A Discourse on the 70th Anniversary of DCLA," *DCLib* 36 (Jan. 1965):4–6; and Joseph W. Rogers, "The Nineties Were Not Really Gay: Notes on DCLA's 75th Anniversary," *DCLib* 40 (Fall 1969):63–70.

The invitation and accounts of the first meetings are in the record book for 1894–1921 in the DCLA Archives. The Cutter letter is in volume 3, which covers the years 1932–34. The Spofford quotation comes from *The Washington Post*'s account of the 6 June meeting, published on 7 June 1894 ("Meeting of Librarians: Local Custodians of Books Take Steps to Form a Club.") The Washington *Evening Star* also reported on the meeting on 7 June under the headlines "Librarians to Organize; Preliminary Meeting of Those in Charge of Local Libraries; A Committee Appointed to Prepare a Plan of Organization—Librarian Spofford and Copyright Books."

## 3. A PUBLIC LIBRARY FOR THE DISTRICT OF COLUMBIA

The book of minutes for 1894–1921 describes association actions on behalf of the library movement.

The Board of Trade quote is from *Report of the Committee on Public Library of the Washington Board of Trade* (1894):5–6; this twelve-page document is a cogent and passionate statement on behalf of the free public library as "an educating and civilizing agent." The characterization of the DCLA committee is from a report published by DCLA secretary Oliver L. Fassig in *The Library Journal* 19 (Nov. 1894):384–85. The story of General Greely's efforts, including the 20 March 1896 quote, is from William A. De Caindry, "The Washington City Free Library," *Records of the Columbia Historical Society*, 16 (1913):64–95. The article on "Libraries of Washington" in *A History of the City of Washington: Its Men and Institutions* by the Washington Post, ed. by Allan B. Slauson (1903) provides useful background information. Spofford's importance to the D.C. Public Library in its formative years is described in Theodore W. Noyes, "Dr. Spofford and the Public Library of the District," in the DCLA publication *Ainsworth Rand Spofford, 1825–1908; A Memorial Meeting* (1909):36–39.

Margaret L. King's unpublished master's degree dissertation, "Beginnings and Early History of the Public Library of the District of Columbia, 1896–1904," is a useful source about the origins of the library and the accomplishments of Weston Flint, its first librarian. An overview of the history of the D.C. Public Library is found in Hardy R. Franklin, "Washington. District of Columbia Public Library," *Encyclopedia of Library and Information Science*, 32 (1981). A survey of the library's history and the story of the Carnegie Building can be found in Alison K. Hoagland,

"The Carnegie Library: The City Beautiful Comes to Mt. Vernon Square," *Washington History* (Fall/ Winter 1990–1991):75–89.

### 4. Professional Interests and Activities, 1894–1945.

This chapter draws on Seabrook, "A Chronological Account of DCLA Meetings, 1894–1954," 97–127, and on meeting notices since 1954 in *D.C. Libraries*, *Intercom*, and in the notebooks of DCLA presidents in the DCLA Archives. Constance McLauglin Green mentions the reading rooms and employees of the Library of Congress and the D.C. Public Library on pp. 129 and 201–203 of her *The Secret City: A History of Race Relations in the Nation's Capital* (1967). Bowerman's advice to future program planners is in his "The District of Columbia Library Association: Semicentennial Notes," *DCLib* 15 (June, for January & April 1944):9–10. Helen T. Steinbarger's comments are in the same issue on page 8. Bernard Green's description of Spofford in the old Library of Congress is in a report in *The Library Journal* 22 (Nov. 1897):708.

### 5. Publications

The DCLA Archives contains a complete set of the association's publications. Seabrook provides details about the rise of *D.C. Libraries* on pp. 52–53 and 63–64. The board's rationale for ending *D.C.*

*Libraries* is in *Intercom* 1 (July 1971):1.

### 6. DCLA and Other Library Associations

This topic is outlined in Seabrook, 20, 50–51, 74–78. Useful background information about the American library movement and the American Library Association came from Wayne A. Wiegand, *The Politics of an Emerging Profession: The American Library Association, 1876–1917* (1986), and Dennis Thomison, *A History of the American Library Association, 1876–1972* (1978).

### 7. Federal Libraries and Librarians

Jane Rosenberg's *The Nation's Great Library: Herbert Putnam and the Library of Congress 1899–1939*, (1993) is the source of information about the Library of Congress and other federal libraries (pp. 62–64) and the percentage of Library of Congress employees in DCLA (p. 36). DCLA's role in the reclassification of federal library jobs is told in Seabrook, 43–47, and in George Bowerman's "Some Reminiscences," *DCLib* 26 (April 1955):3–7. The letter from Price to Kortendick is in volume 5 of the minutes (1943–1954) in the DCLA Archives. Other sources include: Luther H. Evans, "The Survey of Federal Departmental Libraries," *DCLib* 31 (Jan. 1960): 2–8; Paul Howard, "The Federal Library Committee: Progress and Prospects," *DCLib* 40 (Winter 1969):12–16; and L. Quincy Mumford, J. Lee Westrate, and Paul Howard, "The

Establishment of the Federal Library Committee: A Symposium," *DCLib* 36 (Summer 1965):40–50. The quote about the name change is on p. 45 of the last article cited.

### 8. LIBRARY ISSUES AND LEGISLATIVE ACTION

Background information on federal libraries and on federal aid to libraries is found in Richard M. Leach, "A Broad Look at the Federal Government and Libraries," in *Libraries at Large: Tradition, Innovation, and the National Interest*, ed. by Douglas M. Knight and E. Shepley Nourse (1969):346–386. The dinner for the Civil Service commissioners is described in *DCLib* 7 (July 1936):59. Mrs. Roosevelt's talk was reported in *The Washington Post* and the *Evening Star* on 2 April 1936.

The creation and activities of ALA's Washington office are described in Thomison, *A History of the American Library Association*:162–164; *DCLib* 21 (Jan. 1950):2; *DCLib* 21 (April 1950):3; Julia D. Bennett, "Notes from the A.L.A. Washington Office," *DCLib* 24 (Jan. 1953):18; Julia D. Bennett, "An Anniversary," *DCLib* 26 (April 1955):7–10; and Germaine Krettek, "Problems and Programs of the Washington Office," *DCLib* 32 (April 1961):23–26.

Information about DCLA support for the D.C. Public Library comes from Executive Board Minutes and President's Reports, 1960–1982, and from the January 1984 and February 1985 issues of the newsletter, *D.C. Citizen Advocates for Libraries*, all in the DCLA Archives.

### 9. DCLA AND ITS MEMBERS IN TODAY'S WORLD

The questionnaires and annual reports mentioned in this chapter are in the DCLA Archives. The 1966–67 annual report includes a chart showing DCLA membership growth from 1894–1967. A detailed statement of DCLA objectives, labeled "tentative draft," was published in *DCLib* 38 (Spring 1967):29–34. The interest group lists are taken from DCLA presidents' notebooks in the DCLA Archives and the annual membership issues of *Intercom*, published each autumn. The statement of purpose is from *Intercom*, Vol. 16 (Sept. 1986):1.

# ACKNOWLEDGMENTS

⁂

T HE CENTER FOR THE BOOK in the Library of Congress was established in 1977 to stimulate public interest in books, reading, and libraries and to encourage the study of the role of print culture in society. The organizations that comprise "the community of the book" are an important part of our culture, locally and nationally, and it is a pleasure to be able to present this brief history of the District of Columbia Library Association to a wide audience in DCLA's centennial year.

The publications and projects of the Center for the Book and its state affiliates and national reading promotion partners are supported by contributions from individuals, corporations, and foundations. The center particularly wishes to acknowledge contributions from its three major sponsors in 1993: Encyclopaedia Britannica, Paramount Publishing, and the H. W. Wilson Foundation. For editorial help, I am grateful to Alan Bisbort and Sara Day of the Library of Congress's Publishing Office. And for encouragement, I would like to thank Shirley Loo and Elizabeth Stone.

---

## PHOTO CREDITS

10    Library of Congress (LC)
11    Both: LC
15    Left: LC
      Right: District of Columbia
      Library Association (DCLA)
      Archives, DC Public Library
      (DCPL)
18    LC
19    Left: LC
      Right: Washingtoniana
      Division, DCPL
20    Top: LC

      Bottom: Washingtoniana,
      DCPL
30    LC
32    Copyright *Washington Post*,
      Reprinted by permission of
      DCPL
36    Left: DCLA Archives, DCPL
      Right: LC
37    All: DCLA Archives, DCPL
42    LC
43    LC
45    LC: Harris & Ewing photo

48    Both: DCLA Archives, DCPL
50    Copyright *Washington Post*:
      DCPL
51    Left: DCLA Archives, DCPL
      Right: Courtesy *American
      Libraries*
52    DCPL
55    DCPL: Photo by Nathaniel T.
      White
56    LC: Photo by Jim Higgins
59    DCPL

# APPENDIX I

## DCLA PRESIDENTS, 1894–1994

| | | | |
|---|---|---|---|
| 1894–1895 | Ainsworth Rand Spofford<br>Librarian of Congress | 1905 | Cyrus Adler<br>Librarian, Smithsonian Institution |
| 1896 | Cyrus Adler<br>Librarian, Smithsonian Institution | 1906–1907 | George F. Bowerman<br>Librarian, D.C. Public Library |
| 1897 | William P. Cutter<br>Librarian, Department of Agriculture | 1908–1909 | William Dawson Johnston<br>Librarian, Bureau of Education |
| 1898–1899 | Henry Carrington Bolton<br>Bibliographer | 1910–1911 | William Warner Bishop<br>Superintendent of the Reading Room,<br>Library of Congress |
| 1900 | Howard L. Prince<br>Librarian, Patent Office | 1912–1913 | Paul Brockett<br>Librarian, Smithsonian Institution |
| 1901 | Francis A. Crandall<br>Superintendent of Documents | 1914–1915 | Herman H. B. Meyer<br>Chief Bibliographer, Library of Congress |
| 1902–1903 | Thomas H. Clark<br>Law Librarian, Library of Congress | 1916–1917 | William A. Slade<br>Chief, Periodicals Division,<br>Library of Congress |
| 1904 | Thorvald Solberg<br>Register of Copyrights,<br>Library of Congress | 1918 | William J. Hamilton<br>Assistant Librarian, D.C. Public Library<br>(until April) |

1918     Edith Owen (acting)
Superintendent of Documents Office
(April–November)

1919     Theodore Wesley Koch
Chief, Order Division, Library of
Congress (until July)

1919     A. K. Blessing
Assistant Librarian, D. C. Public Library
(July–October)

1920–1921     Herbert Putnam
Librarian of Congress

1922–1923     Dorsey W. Hyde, Jr.
U. S. Chamber of Commerce

1924     Miles O. Price
Librarian, Patent Office

1925–1927     Clara W. Herbert
Assistant Librarian, D.C. Public Library

1927–1929     Frederick W. Ashley
Chief Assistant Librarian,
Library of Congress

1929–1930     Claribel Barnett
Head Librarian, Department of
Agriculture Library

1930–1932     Elizabeth O. Cullen
Reference Librarian,
Bureau of Railway Economics

1932–1933     W. Taylor Purdum
Chief, Acquisitions Department,
D.C. Public Library

1933–1935     Isabel DuBois
Librarian, Bureau of Navigation

1935–1937     John T. Vance
Law Librarian, Library of Congress

1937–1938     Adelaide R. Hasse
Bibliographer, Works Progress
Administration

1938–1939     Ralph L. Thompson
Central Librarian, D.C. Public Library

1939–1940     Elsie Rackstraw
Librarian, Board of Governors,
Federal Reserve System

1940–1942     John Russell Mason
Librarian, George Washington
University Library

1942–1944     David C. Mearns
Director, Reference Department,
Library of Congress

1944–1945     Helen T. Steinbarger
Consultant in Adult Education,
D.C. Public Library

1945–1947     David J. Haykin
Chief, Subject Cataloging Division,
Library of Congress

1947–1948    Paul Howard
             Director, American Library Association
             National Relations Office

1948–1949    Scott Adams
             Army Medical Library

1949–1951    Helen Wessells
             International Information and
             Educational Exchange Program,
             Department of State

1951–1952    Helen Scanlon
             Systems Librarian, Joint Library of the
             International Monetary Fund and the
             International Bank for Reconstruction
             and Development

1952–1954    James J. Kortendick
             Head, Department of Library Science,
             Catholic University

1954–1955    Lucile M. Morsch
             Deputy Chief Assistant Librarian,
             Library of Congress

1955–1956    Louise O. Bercaw
             Assistant Director, Department of
             Agriculture Library

1956–1957    Legare H. B. Obear
             Chief, Loan Division, Library of Congress

1957–1958    Marietta Daniels
             Librarian, Columbus Memorial Library,
             Pan American Union

1958–1959    Lucile Dudgeon
             Librarian, Regional Library of the
             U. S. Information Agency

1959–1960    Robert S. Bray
             Chief, Division for the Blind,
             Library of Congress

1960–1961    Eleanor R. Hastings
             Head, Descriptive Cataloging,
             National Library of Medicine

1961–1962    George B. Moreland
             Director, Public Libraries of
             Montgomery County, MD

1962–1963    Werner B. Ellinger
             Senior Subject Cataloger, Subject
             Cataloging Division, Library of
             Congress

1963–1964    Ruth Fine
             Librarian, Bureau of the Budget Library

1964–1965    Joseph W. Rogers
             Chief Cataloging Division, Copyright
             Office, Library of Congress

1965–1966    Kanardy W. Taylor
             Department of Health,
             Education, and Welfare

1966–1967    Elizabeth W. Stone
             Dean, School of Library and Informa-
             tion Science, Catholic University

1967–1968 Edward M. Waters
Assistant Chief, Music Division,
Library of Congress

1968–1969 Alice Ball
Executive Director, U.S. Book Exchange

1969–1970 Elizabeth L. Tate
Chief, Library Division,
National Bureau of Standards

1970–1971 Richard K. Burns
Director, Falls Church Public Library,
Virginia

1971–1972 Mary A. Huffer
Assistant Director, Smithsonian
Institution Libraries; Director,
Department of the Interior Libraries
(beginning 2/19/72)

1972–1973 Rupert C. Woodward
Director,
George Washington University Library

1973–1974 Paul L. Berry
Director, Reference Department,
Library of Congress

1974–1975 Wallace C. Olsen
Deputy Director, National Agricultural
Library

1975–1976 William L. Whitesides
Director of Libraries, Fairfax County
Public Library, Virginia

1976–1977 Marilyn Gell
Chief of Library Programs, Metropolitan
Washington Council of Governments

1977–1978 Cathy Jones
Head, Reader Services,
George Washington University Library

1978–1979 Lillamaud Hammond
Head of Circulation, Public Services,
Georgetown University Library

1979–1980 Nancy E. Gwinn
Program Officer, Council on Library
Resources, Inc.

1980–1981 Murray Howder
Associate Director, ERIC Document
Processing Facility

1981–1982 Martha Bowman
Associate Director,
George Washington University Library

1982–1983 Judith A. Sessions
Director, Mount Vernon College Library

1983–1984 Darrell Lemke
Coordinator of Library Programs,
Consortium of Universities of the
Washington Metropolitan Area

1984–1985 Lawrence E. Molumby
Deputy Director, D.C. Public Library

1985–1986  Lelia Saunders
Director, Arlington County Public
Library, Virginia

1986–1987  Jacque–Lynne Schulman
Head, Circulation and Control Section,
National Library of Medicine

1987–1988  Molly Raphael
Assistant to the Director,
D.C. Public Library

1988–1989  William Gordon
Director, Prince George's County
Memorial Library System, Maryland

1989–1990  Shirley Loo
Specialist in Information Control and
Automated Systems, Congressional
Research Service, Library of Congress

1990–1991  Doria Beachell Grimes
Product Manager, Bibliographic Data
Bases, National Technical Information
Service

1991–1992  Susan Fifer Canby
Director, National Geographic
Society Library

1992–1993  Hardy R. Franklin
Director, D.C. Public Library

1993–1994  Sue Uebelacker
Branch Manager, Prince George's
County Memorial Library System

1994–1995  Trellis C. Wright
Special Assistant to the Register of
Copyrights, Library of Congress

DCLA PUBLICATIONS, 1894–1994

A SELECTIVE LIST

Library Association of Washington City. *Handbook; with Notes on Libraries in Washington*. Washington, Judd and Detweiler, Printers, 1897. 33 pp.
___*Supplement*, 1898. 16 pp.
___*Supplement*, 1900. 10 pp.

U.S. Library of Congress. *A Union List of Periodicals, Transactions, and Allied Publications Currently Received in the Principal Libraries of the District of Columbia*; compiled under the direction of A. P. C. Griffin. Washington: Government Printing Office, 1901.

District of Columbia Library Association. *Handbook, February 1904*. Washington, Judd and Detweiler, Printers, 1904. 26 pp.

District of Columbia Library Association. *Ainsworth Rand Spofford, 1825–1908; A Memorial Meeting at the Library of Congress on Thursday, November 12, 1908, at Four o'Clock, the Librarian of Congress Presiding*. Printed for the District of Columbia Library Association by The Webster Press, New York City, 1909. 84 pp.

U.S. Library of Congress. Division of Bibliography. *Handbook of the Libraries in the District of Columbia*. Compiled by H. H. B. Meyer, Chief Bibliographer, in cooperation with the D.C. Library Association. Washington, Government Printing Office, 1914. 64 pp.

District of Columbia Library Association. *D.C.L.A. Doings*. Washington, Oct. 1922–March 1926. Published irregularly.

District of Columbia Library Association. *Brief and Specifications for Library Service in the Federal Government*. Submitted to the Personnel Classification Board by the Committee of Government Librarians (Miles O. Price, Chairman). Washington: District of Columbia Library Association, 1923. 94 pp.

District of Columbia Library Association. *Washington's Facilities for Training in Library Science; a Report by the Committee on Library Training*. (Clara W. Herbert, Chairman). Washington, 1923. 12 pp.

District of Columbia Library Association. *Handbook of Washington's Informational Resources*, ed. by

Dorsey W. Hyde, Jr. and Miles O. Price. Washington: District of Columbia Library Association, 1928.

Bowerman, George F. *The New Biography*. Washington, District of Columbia Library Association, 1929. 12 pp.

District of Columbia Library Association. *D.C. Libraries*. Quarterly. Oct. 1929 (vol. 1, no. 1) - Spring 1970 (vol. 41, no. 2).

Roosevelt, Eleanor. *What Libraries Mean to the Nation*. An Address Given at the District of Columbia Library Association Dinner, Carlton Hotel, Washington, D.C., April 1, 1936. Published for the District of Columbia Library Association by the American Library Association. Chicago, April 1936. 7 pp.

*Handbook and Directory*. Published by the Association with the cooperation of the Library of Congress. Washington, 1954. 22 pp.

District of Columbia Library Association. *Clips and Quotes*. July 1966 (vol. 1, no. 1) - May 1970 (vol. IV, no. 5). Occasional newsletter.

District of Columbia Library Association. *Intercom*. July, 1971–.

District of Columbia Library Association. *Specialists' Choice: Important Reference Works in the mid-1970s, Compiled by the DCLA Reference Roundtable*. Washington, 1975. 46 pp.

District of Columbia Library Association. *Washington Area Library Directory*. First Edition. Compiled and Edited by a Committee of Volunteers, David Shumaker, Chair. Washington, D.C.: District of Columbia Library Assocation, 1992. 180 pp.

DCLA AWARDS, 1978–1994

AINSWORTH RAND SPOFFORD PRESIDENT'S AWARD

Named for DCLA's first president, the Spofford Award recognizes an individual or an organization for an outstanding contribution to the entire library community.

| NAME: | DATE OF BOARD ACTION: |
|---|---|
| Elizabeth W. Stone | 1990 |
| Eileen D. Cooke | 1991 |
| David E. Shumaker | 1993 |
| Bernadine A. Hoduski | 1994 |

DISTINGUISHED SERVICE AWARD

The DCLA Distinguished Service Award recognizes a current member for an outstanding contribution to the association.

| NAME: | DATE OF BOARD ACTION: |
|---|---|
| Murray Howder | 1988 |

| NAME: | DATE OF BOARD ACTION: |
|---|---|
| Darrell Lemke | 1989 |
| Shirley Loo | 1991 |
| Mary K. Feldman | 1992 |
| Susan Fifer Canby | 1993 |
| Kathryn Ray | 1994 |

AWARDS FOR SPECIAL ASSISTANCE

| NAME: | DATE OF BOARD ACTION: |
|---|---|
| President Jimmy Carter and Mrs. Carter | 1978 |
| Paul L. Berry | 1980 |
| Mary K. Feldman | 1983 |
| Shirley Loo | 1983 |

# APPENDIX IV

## AMERICAN LIBRARY ASSOCIATION TRIBUTE RESOLUTION HONORING THE DISTRICT OF COLUMBIA LIBRARY ASSOCIATION ON THE OCCASION OF ITS 100TH ANNIVERSARY

WHEREAS:

the District of Columbia Library Association (DCLA) was founded on June 15, 1894; and

WHEREAS:

the first President of DCLA was Ainsworth Rand Spofford, the sixth Librarian of Congress; and

WHEREAS:

DCLA has been a chapter of the American Library Association since 1922; and

WHEREAS:

numerous DCLA members have served as president of the American Library Association, including William Warner Bishop, Herman H. B. Meyer, Lucile M. Morsch, Herbert Putnam, Elizabeth W. Stone, Patricia Wilson Berger, and Hardy R. Franklin; and

WHEREAS:

Legislative Day was initiated by DCLA in 1975; and

WHEREAS:

its members have been committed to promoting and supporting libraries and information centers in Washington, D.C. and the greater metropolitan area; and

WHEREAS:

DCLA has successfully promoted professional development, continuing education, and collegial exchange among librarians and information specialists; and

WHEREAS:

DCLA started the Continuing Education Workshops which evolved into the highly successful Joint Spring Workshops (now cosponsored by other local library organizations) and which have benefitted thousands of librarians (and were initiated by distinguished members Eileen D. Cooke and Dr. Elizabeth W. Stone); and

WHEREAS:

the DCLA has supported library school students by loaning over $7,000 through the DCLA Student Loan Fund; now, therefore, be it

RESOLVED:

That the Council of the American Library Association extends its congratulations to the members of the District of Columbia Library Association on the occasion of its centennial anniversary; and, be it further

RESOLVED:

That the Council of the American Library Association expresses to the members of DCLA its encouragement and best wishes for the next 100 years.

---

*This resolution, designated Tribute #5, was approved by the Council of the American Library Association at its 1994 midwinter meeting. It was introduced by DCLA Chapter Councilor Robert R. Newlen and seconded by Virginia Chapter Councilor Tom Hehman and Sandy Stephan, Maryland Chapter Councilor.*

# APPENDIX V

LIST OF DCLA CENTENNIAL MEMBERS

These DCLA members showed their support for
the organization by enlisting as centennial members
for 1993–1994

Anderson, Blanche
Austin, Rhea
Avery, Gail W.
Baxter, William E.
Beaufort, Jennifer
Berger, Patricia Wilson
Berry, Paul L.
Boyd, Maurice
Brown, Charles
Carter, Constance
Clemmer, Dan
Cole, John Y.
Conaty, Barbara
Cooke, Eileen D.
Cornelius, John C.
Craigwell, Jean
Dickson, Constance
Drewes, Arlene
Eppink, Alice
Farley, Judith
Feldman, Mary
Fields, Patti
Fifer Canby, Susan

Fine, Ruth
Finkler, Norman
Forstall, Louise D.
Franklin, Hardy R.
Glick, Warren
Gordon, William
Grimes, Doria Beachell
Gwinn, Nancy E.
Hale, Elizabeth
Haley, Roger
Hays, Janet
Heanue, Anne
Henderson, Carol
Hendrickson, Norma K. R.
Hill, Susan M.
Hill, Victoria
Hoduski, Bernadine
Howder, Murray
Hussey, Sandra
Ivory, Edrice
Iyer, Thangam R.
Knauff, Elisabeth S.
Krell, H. Barbara

Lemke, Darrell
Levering, Mary Berghaus
Loewinger, Margaret
Loo, Shirley
Mahar, Ellen
Mansfield, Jerry
Masters, Deborah C.
McDonald, Lynn
McElroy, Elizabeth
Missar, Charles D.
Missar, Margaret Mary
Mohr, Diane
Molumby, Lawrence E.
Morland, Barbara
Mumford, Carole
New, Gregory
Newlen, Robert
Noyes, Pamela
Phelps, Thomas
Platt, Suzy
Platz, Valerie Anna
Pourron, Eleanor
Preer, Jean

Raphael, Molly
Ray, Kathryn
Reid, Judith P.
Reynolds, Dennis J.
Roberts, Barbara
Robinson, Barbara
Rosen, Janice
Sadak, Luz
Schaaf, Robert
Schubel, Maura Dolan
Schulman, Jacque-Lynne
Schwartz, Marla

Scott, Kathryn S.
Smith, Barbara J.
Smutko, Charlotte
Snyder, Hila
Solomon, Fern Rice
Stone, Elizabeth W.
Tate, Elizabeth L.
Taylor, Joan
Ternes, Mary C.
Thompson, Elizabeth M.
Thompson-Joyner, Rita S.
Trautman, Maryellen

Uebelacker, Sue
Walther, James H.
Wand, Patricia
Waters, Lily
Williams, Maurvene D.
Willis, H. Warren
Willis, Maria Clara
Woodall, Nancy
Wright, Trellis C.
Young, Christina

COLOPHON

TYPE
*Adobe™ Goudy and Goudy Oldstyle*

COMPOSITION
*Created electronically using QuarkXPress®*
*on the Apple® Macintosh® computer*
*by Inglis Design*

COVER PAPER
*Strathmore Grandee, Kimono Red, 80 lb.*

TEXT PAPER
*Mohawk Opaque, Cream, Smooth finish, 80 lb.*

PRINTING
*Bruce Printing, Incorporated*
*Forestville, Maryland*

DESIGN
*Patricia Inglis*